The *Wisest* Investment

The *Wisest* Investment

TEACHING YOUR KIDS *to*
Be RESPONSIBLE, INDEPENDENT
and MONEY-SMART *for* LIFE

Robin Taub

CPA, CA

ISBN 978-1-7774484-0-0

The following information is intended as a general reference tool for understanding the underlying principles and practices of the subject matter covered. The opinions and ideas expressed herein are solely those of the author. The author and publisher are not engaged in rendering legal, accounting, tax, insurance, financial, investment or other professional advice or services in this publication. The publication is not intended to provide a basis for action in particular circumstances without consideration by a competent professional. The strategies outlined in this book may not be suitable for every individual, and are not guaranteed or warrantied to produce any particular results. Further, any examples or sample forms presented are intended only as illustrations.

The author, publisher and their agents assume no responsibility for errors or omissions and expressly disclaim any responsibility for any liability, loss or risk, personal or otherwise, which is incurred as a consequence, directly or indirectly, of the use and application of any of the contents of this book.

The first edition of this book, *A Parent's Guide to Raising Money-Smart Kids*, was originally published by the Canadian Institute of Chartered Accountants, now CPA Canada. The second edition, *Raising Money-Smart Kids: How to Teach Your Kids About Money While Learning a Few Things Yourself*, was published by CPA Canada and Cormorant Books Inc., under license. No endorsement of this edition by CPA Canada is implied.

Edited by: Erik Leijon
Interior design: Jessica Albert
Cover design: David A. Gee

If you're interested in bulk purchases of *The Wisest Investment*, we offer an aggressive discount schedule.

All inquiries should be addressed to:

The Wisest Investment
1210 Eglinton Ave West
Toronto, ON, M6C 2E3

books@robintaub.com; (416) 256-4498
www.thewisestinvestment.com

Printed in Canada

Dedicated to Justin and Natalie,
my wisest investments!

Introduction

Like most parents, you feel a responsibility to teach your kids about money. You understand the importance of making sound financial decisions and developing good financial habits. You know how financial struggles can strain relationships and even take a toll on your health. But teaching kids about money is easier said than done, especially in today's financially complex, digital world where the tools we use are constantly changing to keep pace.

At a time when cash is disappearing, spending is frictionless, and fraud and scams are constant threats, seemingly out of nowhere, COVID-19 hit. Its sudden and devastating impact on the economy accelerated and magnified these trends. Many families found themselves financially unprepared, and the pandemic served as a wake-up call about the importance of teaching the next generation about money.

According to research, most parents feel they don't have the information they need to teach the right lessons about money, and they don't know how to approach the subject with kids of different ages. But they do recognize they need help, and they are willing to listen and learn.

As a Chartered Professional Accountant, I've always felt comfortable and confident around money and financial concepts. And I believe money management is an important life skill, one that I wanted to pass on to my two kids. So in 2011, when I was asked to write a book to help parents teach their kids about money, I was intrigued. I had just started writing for the Ontario Securities Commission's financial literacy website, getsmarteraboutmoney.ca. But writing a book? It wasn't something I had ever really thought about doing. It certainly wasn't on my bucket list (like meeting Bruce Springsteen, which I managed to do in 2007!).

When Justin and Natalie were young, I started to invest in their financial education. I knew that the earlier kids are taught about money, the greater the likelihood of financial success throughout their lives. I tried to put my money where my mouth was and be a good financial role model to them. I took advantage of teachable moments to build money lessons into our daily lives, and I made sure that the information I shared with them (about earning, saving, spending, sharing and investing) was appropriate for their age and maturity (and I still do). Back in 2011, when my kids were 14 and 16, I could already see my efforts were paying off.

After some reflection, I thought to myself, *Maybe*

I do have a book in me! Why not write about my own experiences — both rewarding and challenging — and the experiences of other parents? That, combined with solid research, would help parents like you give *your* kids the knowledge, skills and confidence that I gave my own kids.

I wrote *A Parent's Guide to Raising Money-Smart Kids*, and it quickly became a Canadian bestseller. In the decade since it was first published, society has moved away from cash toward mobile and digital money and the economic consequences of the coronavirus pandemic have only accelerated this move. This third, updated version builds on time-tested lessons that have always applied and still apply today, while modifying some for the post-pandemic "new normal." It also addresses both the challenges and benefits of managing money in an increasingly digital world. Over the same decade, my kids have grown into financially literate, independent and responsible young adults (most of the time!).

For anyone who may be thinking, *How can I teach my kids about money if I'm not doing a good job of it myself?*, this book will make you more aware of your own behaviour around money and the type of financial role model you are to your kids now (and the type of role model you can become). But it's something you and your kids can learn together, and it may even lead to improvements in your own financial habits and health as you become more skilled in understanding, practising and explaining money management.

To get the most out of your reading, you should

understand a few things about how I've organized the book. The first chapter sets the stage, explaining why teaching your kids about money is the wisest investment. It also covers what that implies about your own responsibility to be smart with your money so that you can teach by example.

But beyond your own example, there is the very basic need to talk to your kids about money. How do you approach it? Well, there are five pillars of money that can be used to structure an ongoing conversation. Chapter 1 explains the fact that in order to have money you have to earn it. Then, once you've earned it, there are just four things to do with it:

- save
- spend
- share
- invest

Chapters 2 through 5 are directed at parents with kids at different stages:

- young children (ages 5–8)
- preteens (ages 9–12)
- teens (ages 13–17)
- emerging adults (ages 18–21)

Each chapter is organized around the five pillars of money just discussed — **earn**, **save**, **spend**, **share**, and **invest** — and explores specific topics within each. There are suggestions for family discussions and activities designed to reinforce these concepts. Each chapter also contains quotes from parents talking about how they approached financial education with their kids, which remind us that we can find humour in even the most serious of subjects.

I hope the suggestions in this book and the real-life experiences of other parents will help you make the wisest investment. I would love to hear from you. Please email me at wisestinvestment@robintaub.com.

Robin

Contents

The Wisest Investment

Teaching Your Kids about Money

This first chapter explains why teaching your kids about money is the wisest investment and helps you understand the context in which kids learn about money. It discusses some of the problem areas that parents run into and suggests approaches to deal with those problems effectively. This chapter also introduces the Eleven Healthy Habits of Financial Management, which can help you achieve two objectives: getting your own finances in order and teaching your kids how to do the same.

Why Is Teaching Your Kids about Money the Wisest Investment?

We want our kids to thrive in life. We want them to be able to manage their lives well, including their financial lives, for their sakes as well as our own. If we don't succeed in teaching our kids about money management, it may come back to haunt us. How would you feel, for instance, if you had to support your adult children financially? (Most Canadians can't afford to.) Or if you had to bail them out of a financial mess, like bankruptcy or an expensive divorce, with savings painstakingly accumulated and set aside for your own future? What if this happened when you were supposed to be enjoying your carefree retirement years? It's not a pretty picture, is it?

Those are some of the potential consequences for us as parents, but what about the kids themselves? If you've ever struggled with financial problems that were brought on by bad habits — or simply by not knowing how to approach financial management effectively and efficiently — then you know what a negative impact such problems can have on your life generally, and especially on your relationships with the people closest to you. Money stress can even be bad for your health and is a common cause of anxiety and depression. It's certainly worth investing in our children to spare them from such struggles.

The Canadian government felt that financial literacy was critical to Canadian economic growth and prosperity, and they created a task force to study it in 2009. The task force defined financial literacy as having the knowledge, skills, and confidence to make responsible decisions at every life stage. Many people now recognize it as an important life skill.

"A neighbour has a 26-year-old daughter who lives at home with her parents. She only has a part-time job working in retail. She Ubers everywhere rather than take public transit, goes out for brunch every weekend, buys takeout food regularly for dinner, and before the pandemic hit, had just came home from a week's vacation in Mexico. She doesn't have any savings at all — no RRSP, no TFSA, not even a basic savings account, and now she doesn't have a job. The worst part is, she couldn't care less about learning about finances — she's more concerned about how many followers she has on Instagram! Her parents now bemoan the fact that they did not take the time to teach their daughter good money management skills and habits when she was younger. They're distressed by the fact that she doesn't seem to share any of their values and seems to take so much for granted. It's really strained their relationship with her."

Healthy, happy and successful adults, among other things, are adults who are financially responsible and independent. That's the goal for our children as they become young adults, but it's normal to encounter bumps along the road. For example, in challenging economic times, your kids may need a little more support. When youth unemployment is at record high levels, twentysomething children may want to move (or stay) home, in order to build savings, or avoid getting (further) into debt. Or if they are employed, they may need help paying for a car to get to work safely. This support shouldn't come at the cost of your own financial well-being, and every family has to decide what feels right for them.

What Are the Challenges Parents Face?

The basic challenges parents face when trying to teach their kids about money are lack of knowledge, lack of time, and lack of opportunity (or not always recognizing when an opportunity presents itself). Teaching your kids how to manage money is particularly hard if you're not good at it yourself. It becomes easy to just avoid the conversations altogether, especially when you're running a busy household with so many competing demands on your time. Although it may not feel like a priority when your kids are little, their early years are an important time to lay the foundation and teach the basics. The concepts are the same as they get older, but the stakes get much higher. It's better if they can learn from their mistakes when the stakes are low.

A lot of parents procrastinate: they don't teach their kids about money because they think their kids are too young. But there are lots of ways to engage younger children with money. Maybe your kids don't seem all that interested in learning about money. Your challenge is to make it relevant to them and to use opportunities in your everyday lives as teachable moments. You don't have to set aside extra time; these opportunities will crop up in day-to-day activities like grocery shopping (either in-store or online) and opening a bank account, as well as when your kids get their first real job.

What if your kids are already teenagers, but you've never taught them about money: is it too late? No — it's never too late to learn a new skill or to learn how to do things better. The way you approach money management with teens is different. For instance, you can discuss more sophisticated topics with them than with their younger siblings, but the basic concepts are the same throughout your kids' lives and your own. When you earn money, you have four basic choices about what to do with it: save, spend, share, and invest. You want your kids to understand that making a lot of money doesn't guarantee financial security; financial security comes from making sound decisions with the money you make.

Financial technology (known as "fintech") is changing every aspect of how we deal with money and has produced new ways to manage it in a digital and mobile world. Much of what we do with money (whether we are earning, saving, spending, donating, or investing) can increasingly be done using technology, either online or on our phones. Canada (along with the rest of the world) is moving toward a cashless society. In Sweden, before the pandemic, 98 percent of transactions were digital, and they have almost eliminated cash. So how do you teach your kids about money in an increasingly cash-free world, which the pandemic has only accelerated?

The answer, especially with younger kids, still starts with cold, hard cash. As your kids get older, you can introduce "paying with plastic" (i.e., debit and credit cards) and from there move on to digital money and tools like apps. We will address this issue in more detail in subsequent chapters.

Who's Teaching Your Kids about Money?

When asked who should be responsible for educating children about responsible money management, most respondents in a study conducted by CPA Canada (CICA Canadian Finance Study 2010) felt that parents or guardians had the most responsibility. Next in line were schools, followed by the financial services industry and then government. We'll get to the very important role that parents play in the next section, but first a word about financial literacy in school.

FINANCIAL LITERACY IN SCHOOL

Each province is responsible for whether and how financial literacy is taught in school. For example, financial literacy has been integrated into the curriculum in Ontario from Grades 4 to 12 since 2011. This means it's being taught in many different subjects such as math, social studies, Canadian and world studies, business studies, and others. Students learn about basic money management and how to be an educated consumer, and they gain knowledge that will help them be confident in making decisions about where and how to invest their money.

Other studies[1] have shown that 84 percent of parents and 70 percent of high school students want financial learning in the classroom. Beginning in 2019, Ontario's new career studies curriculum for Grade 10 took a deeper look at financial management, including budgeting for the first year after graduation and comparing different forms of borrowing to pay for post-secondary education.[2]

In 2008, the British Columbia Securities Commission (BCSC) and the Financial Consumer Agency of Canada adapted an existing BCSC resource called Planning 10: The City into a national online resource called The City/La Zone. It gives youth the knowledge, skills, and confidence to plan for their post-secondary education or career and to navigate through the financial realities of adulthood.

A 2017 PricewaterhouseCoopers study found that millennials (the generation born between the early 1980s and the mid-1990s) are generally better educated and more skilled than their parents were at the

---

1. See Ontario Securities Commission: getsmarteraboutmoney.ca.
2. www.cbc.ca/news/canada/toronto/grade-10-career-studies-curriculum-focus-financial-literacy-ontario-1.5197517

same age, but only 24 percent have basic financial literacy (meaning an understanding of assets, expenses, and income). Just 8 percent have high financial literacy, including a grasp of taxes, mortgages, and investing. In response, some universities in Canada are offering personal finance courses.

For example, McGill University is offering a free, online, personal finance essentials course, which covers budgeting, borrowing, real estate and more. Taught by professors from the Desautels Faculty of Management, the course is open to everyone.

L'Université du Québec à Trois-Rivières offers a massive open online course on personal finance. The free, five-week online class covers personal finance basics, taxes and tax breaks, and growing your personal wealth.

So ask your kids what they're learning in school about money and try to reinforce those lessons at home.

What Kind of Financial Role Model Are You?

As parents, you try to be good role models for your children. You're careful about how you treat and relate to others, how you look after your health and well-being, and how you balance work and family life, because you know your kids observe everything. They're watching and learning from you — and they pick up both your good and bad habits, including habits of financial management. So what kind of financial role model are you?

- Do you spend money impulsively or are you cautious and deliberate about your spending?
- Do you save up for a big purchase or do you buy what you want when you want it, charge it to your credit card, and worry about it later?
- Do you pay your bills on time and keep organized files or do you delete them, unread, from your inbox?

Try doing the **Role Model Self-Assessment** exercise at the end of this chapter; it will give you a good idea of where you stand as a role model. And if you teach your kids well, you'll find that older siblings can also be important role models for younger kids.

IS MONEY A TABOO TOPIC IN YOUR HOME?

"I was 11 when my father sat me down for 'the talk.' My father never did actually explain how sex worked, I think he thought a person just naturally figured that out. Money was different. Money was something that needed explaining."

— Michael Lewis, Against the Rules podcast, season 1, episode 7

In many households, money is a taboo topic. Many parents say they avoid talking about money with their kids because they don't feel qualified to do it properly. They don't know how to approach it, and they don't have the information they need. Many also feel they're not equipped to handle some of the uncomfortable questions that their kids may ask in normal times, like "Are we rich?" or "How much money do you make?"

But with many Canadians struggling financially and facing uncertain futures caused by the economic fallout of COVID-19, they may be getting questions right now like "Can we pay our rent/mortgage?" or "When are you going back to work?" The answers to these kinds of questions are private family matters and probably not something you want to share with the whole world, so you have to keep in mind your child's age, maturity and temperament when answering them. Ask your kid questions to make sure you understand what they're really asking. Often, when kids ask such questions, they're really just looking for reassurance that everything's okay, even though no one knows for certain what the "new normal" will look like. But if they ask, it's best to find an answer that is honest, one that stresses confidentiality and trust, and one that is only as detailed as you think appropriate. The discussion can often take place by dealing with general concepts rather than getting into specific numbers — concepts such as:

- the meaning of "rich";
- the importance of income, i.e., not that it

should be a certain amount, but that it's sufficient to provide a stable life;
- how mortgages work; and
- good debt versus bad debt.

While it may be taboo to expose confidential family information, there should be nothing distasteful about teaching your kids general money management skills. Living within your means, budgeting, and saving for important goals should be discussed openly — and they should be discussed often.

THE BIG PICTURE: HOUSEHOLD FINANCES

One of the goals of teaching your kids about money is to make them aware of the cost of running a household. Not that your kids should feel responsible for making ends meet — that's your job as a head of the household. But they can at least become aware of the costs of their needs and wants and get a better understanding of how providing for them fits into the bigger picture. Kids, especially teenagers, can seem selfish because they tend to focus only on their own needs and wants. With more information, though, they will come to realize that you have to prioritize and balance all of the family's costs of living. It helps them put things in the proper perspective.

BUDGETING: OVERHEAD EXPENSES AND DISCRETIONARY SPENDING

Raising kids is expensive. According to the website MoneySense, the estimated cost of raising a child in Canada from birth to adulthood (in today's dollars) is approximately $13,366 a year or just over $250,000 — and these costs are just some of the components of your household budget. For some families, budgeting is a dreaded activity, right up there with dieting! Both words bring up thoughts of deprivation. But if you think of a budget as a spending plan, one that will let you have and do the things in life that are most important to you and that are aligned with your values, it makes an otherwise tedious process meaningful and rewarding.

When creating a spending plan, keep in mind that your expenses fall into two broad categories: overhead expenses and discretionary spending. Most overhead expenses are fixed costs and are governed by a contract. They're easier to plan for than variable expenses because they usually cost the same amount every month (though some fixed costs, such as annual home insurance premiums, are periodic or occasional). These expenses can't really be avoided because they're the basic costs of living. Examples of overhead expenses are:

- rent or mortgage payments;
- property taxes;
- child care/daycare;
- car payments or other transportation costs; and
- cable, internet, or cell phone bills.

Other overhead expenses like groceries, clothing, utilities, and gas for the car are a bit more variable — the amount you spend may change from month to month — but you can't eliminate these expenses altogether.

Discretionary expenses, on the other hand, are a lot more flexible. You decide whether to incur these costs at all, and, if you do, how much to spend. Examples include:

- restaurant meals and entertainment;
- recreational shopping;
- personal care;
- vacations;
- club dues;
- hobbies; and
- gifts.

So how do you budget? The initial step is to pay yourself first by automatically transferring a certain sum of money every month to a designated account. Depending on your goals and objectives, this can be either a regular savings account or a tax-advantaged account like a Registered Retirement Savings Plan (RRSP) or a Tax-Free Savings Account (TFSA). You get used to living without this money, and what remains after you've paid yourself first goes toward covering your overhead expenses. Any funds that remain after you cover all of your overhead expenses are available for discretionary spending or additional savings.

"Don't save what is left after spending; spend what is left after saving."[3]

— WARREN BUFFET

Use the **Cash Flow Calculator** at the end of this chapter to calculate your household cash flow. Most likely, the biggest cash outflow in your budget is your mortgage payment or rent, followed by car payments, property tax, insurance, and possibly tuition. You can use the Cash Flow Calculator to create a spending plan that's right for you and your family.

CLOSING A FINANCIAL GAP

Preparing your budget and your cash flow will give you a clear picture of your financial health. If you're spending less than you earn, your cash flow will be positive. That positive cash flow is money for savings (or sometimes for further discretionary spending). If, on the other hand, you're spending more than you make, your cash flow will be negative. Most people deal with negative cash flow by using credit to cover the shortfall. For example, they may use credit cards, department store cards, personal lines of credit, or home equity lines of

---

3. www.supermoney.com/2014/04/10-powerful-personal-finance-quotes-from-warren-buffett/

credit. Using credit occasionally because your household cash flow is uneven (e.g., you're self-employed or earn commissions) is fine. In those situations, you may run surpluses (excess cash flow) some months and deficits (insufficient cash flow) other months. But if you're using credit every month to make ends meet, then you're living beyond your means. You're also building up debt as those monthly shortfalls begin to accumulate. This situation is obviously not sustainable. In his book, *Client-Centred Life Planning*,[4] Michael R. Curtis introduces the following "Three C" strategies to close a financial gap:

1. **Create:** creating additional income or wealth
2. **Convert:** converting consumption assets into income-producing assets
3. **Conserve:** conserving existing resources

You can use these strategies alone or together. In tough times, this may mean cutting back on spending, selling things you no longer need and stretching existing supplies. Always look for high-leverage solutions that will have a significant impact on the bottom line. For instance, if you can't afford your monthly car payments, conserving by cutting back on your streaming subscription may help a bit, but it probably won't get you all the way there!

---

4. (Toronto, Canada: Michael R. Curtis, 2005).

CREATE

Creating wealth brings more cash into the household. For some people, this may mean returning to the paid labour force, creating a side hustle by turning a passion or hobby into a business, or participating in the gig economy by, for example, driving for Uber. Perhaps you could rent out a spare room or the basement apartment in your house. For others, it may mean adjusting their investment portfolio to focus more on generating income to supplement their salary.

CONVERT

Downsizing to a smaller house is the classic example of the "Convert" strategy and has been a popular strategy as people move into their retirement years. Selling your large family home, buying a less expensive, smaller home, and investing the difference allows you to convert a consumption asset into an income-producing asset. Or leverage the sharing economy by listing your house on Airbnb during periods when you're travelling or living elsewhere. Converting may also involve the sale of a cottage or other vacation property, a boat, a car, or any other unnecessary assets to generate capital that can be invested to produce income or meet other financial objectives.

CONSERVE

Creating and converting are long- and medium-term solutions, but conserving has immediate impact. Examine your expenses for ways to defer, cut back, or eliminate excessive or unnecessary spending. Look for discretionary expenses like meals, entertainment, shopping, and vacations that are easy to cut.

If you take these tips to heart, you can rest assured that you will become exactly the kind of role model your kids need to make them money-smart — both now and throughout their lives.

How Your Values Influence Your Financial Decisions

Values are the things in your life that are most important to you, that you're willing to take a stand for. Some people value education, achievement, prestige, or wealth. Others value security, family, friendship, or adventure. The way you spend your money and deal with your finances says a lot about your values. Do you know what your top five values are? Do the **Values Validator** exercise at the end of this chapter and find out.

You may think your kids will pick up your values by osmosis, but these days kids are exposed to a lot of conflicting messages about money, especially from traditional and social media and their friends. So be clear about your family values and how they impact your financial decisions. Get your kids to try the Values Validator and to leave their answers out in the kitchen where everyone can see them. Let the list be a visual reminder to help all of you to stay focused on your values and the things you're committed to. The values you pass on to your kids will help them prioritize their spending and set meaningful and compelling goals for themselves. The combination of solid values and strong money management skills creates a good foundation for making sound financial and life decisions.

Can Money Buy Happiness?

Many people think that if they had more money, they'd be happier. However, studies have shown that while happiness increases as you earn up to $75,000 a year, after that, making more money doesn't actually make you happier. So once you have enough money to meet your basic needs, how can you use it to make your lives happier?

1. Shift from buying "stuff" for yourself to investing in experiences. Research shows that people tend to be happy with new things initially, until they realize better things are available. Satisfaction with stuff tends to decrease over time, while satisfaction with experiences like travel, hobbies, or concerts and other live events tends to increase with the passage of time. Unfortunately, many of these experiences are on hold until people feel safe being in close proximity again.
2. Spend time and money on others. People who give back and help others who are less fortunate often say they get back more than they give.
3. Spend money to save time. Paying someone to do personal or household chores and tasks can free you up to spend time on the people and things that matter most. It can also buy you time to exercise, an activity that results in immediate and-long-term benefits for happiness.

"Simon, who just turned six, now gets an allowance and is expected to save some of it, spend some, and share some. He decided he wanted to buy himself a toy, so his mother took him to the dollar store. But before he got to the toy, he passed jars of bubbles, which his baby brother, Arthur, adores. He carefully looked at the price and said he wanted to buy those for Arthur. Then he felt sad because he wouldn't be able to buy a toy for himself. His mother explained to him that he had in fact saved enough spend money for both! It made him so happy to spend his own money on a gift for his little brother."

The Eleven Healthy Habits of Financial Management

As we've indicated, becoming a money-smart family starts with developing healthy financial habits and then modelling them for your kids.

Throughout this guide, we will refer to the Taylor family (Robert, Michelle, and their daughter, Emma) as a great example of how to do things right. They have 11 healthy habits for managing their finances — simple, common-sense guidelines that keep their affairs in order and set the stage for any discussions they may want to have with their kid about money. Here they are:

1. Know where you stand financially

The starting point for the Taylors was figuring out their net worth: everything they own less everything they owe. And they keep a close eye on it, making sure it's moving in the right direction, with assets growing and debt shrinking. Why not take the first step in figuring out where you stand by completing the **Net Worth Worksheet** at the end of this chapter?

The Taylors also know how much money comes in every month (and every year). They understand that it's a finite amount, and they treat it with care. Equally important, they understand that managing money is about making choices. Like the rest of us, they have to decide what to do with the money that comes in: how much to save, spend, share, and invest. And they control how much money goes out by monitoring their household cash flow using a template similar to our **Cash Flow Calculator** at the end of this chapter.

2. Live within your means

Arguably, this is the most important lesson you can teach your kids. And the best way to teach it is to actually live this way, to walk the walk. The Taylors simply don't spend more than they make. In fact, they make sure they can't spend more than they make because they always follow the third healthy habit.

3. *Save, or pay yourself first*

Every month, they take a certain amount of money directly from their paycheques and put it into savings. To make sure it happens, and to make it really easy, they set it up as an automatic transfer. They're now used to living without this money, and they spend only what remains. They don't rack up credit card debt or balances on home equity loans or lines of credit because they follow the fourth healthy habit.

4. *Understand the difference between good debt and bad debt*

The Taylors understand that credit can be a wonderful tool when used responsibly. Credit is convenient — much more convenient than using cash or cheques. Credit can also act as a safety net in case of an emergency (more on that in healthy habit 5). Building a good credit history enables you to make big purchases such as a car or a house at a reasonable interest rate; like many families, the Taylors have a mortgage on their house. Incurring debt for the purpose of buying an asset — something that adds to your net worth and has the potential to go up in value, such as a house or a stock — is an example of good debt. Student loan debt is another example of good debt, as it's an investment in the student's future career and earning power.

However, even with good debt, you must never take on more than you can repay within a reasonable period of time. If you have trouble servicing your debt (you pay late or you miss payments), you will damage your credit rating. Bad credit hurts: you may be denied loans or have to pay extremely high interest rates, and you may face higher insurance rates. Some employers even check the credit of prospective employees. They see credit history as an indication of responsibility.

Bad debt, which is something the Taylors actively avoid, is debt incurred to purchase consumption goods such as furniture, appliances, TVs, and clothes. These items have almost no resale value, don't go up in value (in fact, they lose value the minute you walk out of the store with them), and don't add to your net worth. Going into debt on your credit card or department store card to buy these types of items is very costly by the time you factor in the interest expense. The Taylors save up for these types of purchases.

5. Set up a financial safety net

The Taylors want their family to be protected in case a financial emergency occurs. A rule of thumb is to have three to six months' worth of living expenses in cash reserves, because if you become unemployed, that is how long it takes, on average, to find a new job in your field. An emergency fund can also get you through a period when you can't work due to injury or illness. However, because of high levels of household debt, easy access to lines of credit and very low rates of interest on saving accounts, one-third of Canadians didn't have an emergency fund when the pandemic hit. The Taylors, however, do have an adequate emergency fund, that will enable them to keep up their mortgage payments and buy food if one of them suddenly loses their job or otherwise can't work (due to illness, for example). They also have adequate life and disability insurance, as well as automobile and homeowner's insurance.

6. Know the difference between needs and wants

If you want something badly enough, it can be really easy to convince yourself you need it, especially given the very powerful forces in the media that try to convince us that our "wants" are actually "needs." Our kids are bombarded at least as much as we are, if not more, when you consider time spent on social media, and they may lack the critical thinking skills that help us deconstruct the advertisers' methods and messages. We're not doing our kids (or ourselves) any favours by giving in to their every demand.

FAMILY DISCUSSION

Needs versus Wants

Before deciding to make a purchase, ask your kid to answer this question: "Do I really need this, or would it just be nice to have?" You'd be amazed at how much money that simple question can save you! And you might be surprised at your kid's willingness to give it a try.

7. Teach delayed gratification and set financial goals

Delaying gratification is another important life skill you can help your kids develop. A famous psychological study (the "marshmallow test") proved this. It showed the effect of impulse control and willpower on academic, emotional, and social success.

A group of four-year-olds were given marshmallows. They were told that they could have one marshmallow now, but if they could wait several minutes, they could have two. Some children grabbed a marshmallow and ate it. Others waited, some covering their eyes to avoid seeing the tempting treat. One child even licked the table around the marshmallow!

Over 14 years, the researchers followed the group and found that the "grabbers" suffered low self-esteem and were perceived by others as prone to envy and easily frustrated. The "waiters" coped better and were more socially competent, self-assertive, trustworthy, dependable, and academically successful. The lesson: strong willpower and impulse control will help us stay on task and meet our goals throughout our lives, whether it's studying instead of watching TV or saving for retirement instead of spending.

Setting financial goals is one thing you can do that helps teach delayed gratification. And setting goals can be easy.

Just writing them down and being able to see a list or a collage takes away some of the urgency around buying. Waiting for a reward by setting goals in this way — and delaying gratification — also helps to counter any attitude of entitlement your kids may have picked up. Many parents also find they can delay gratification on big-ticket items by connecting them to a special occasion like a birthday, holiday, or other special occasion like graduation.

Sometimes, kids just need reminding that shiny new things lose their lustre pretty quickly. When Emma Taylor was young and was pestering her parents for something she just "had to have," Michelle used to ask her: "Remember the last thing you had to have? What was that again? And do you have any idea where it is?" It was usually somewhere in the corner of their basement playroom gathering dust!

THINGS TO DO

Wish list

Create a wish list of wants with your kids. It can take many forms:

- Make a simple, written list
- Create a "vision board" or collage of images of things your kids want

8. _Track your spending_

There are many different ways to find out where your money is really going. It doesn't matter how you track your spending; the important thing is that you bring awareness to your spending habits. It's a great reality check. You may be shocked to learn that your actual spending bears very little resemblance to how you think you spend your money. You may also find that tracking and reviewing your spending is a powerful motivator to make better spending choices.

If tracking all of your spending seems overwhelming, there is a shortcut you can take: focus on your problem areas. We all have them — those little indulgences that are more want than need. Begin by just monitoring those and asking yourself if you still use that monthly app or delivery subscription, or if you think you can live without it. When you spend out of habit or routine, you rarely ask yourself if you're getting value for your money. But being more mindful of your spending may lead to more informed — and more satisfying — spending choices going forward.

These days, all of the big banks have tracking and budgeting tools built into their mobile banking apps. The app automatically downloads and categorizes your spending, compares your spending to your monthly average, and lets you set up budgets. You can also set up real-time alerts every time there's a transaction, as well as notifications that summarize your daily spending. Research has shown that these technological "nudges" lead to a decline in spending.

The Taylors also take the extra step of comparing their actual spending to their budget to see if they're on track. Because a budget is a work in progress, the Taylors use what they learn to tweak their budget on a regular basis and make it more realistic.

THINGS TO DO

Tracking spending

Which of the following would work best for you?

- Keep a written spending journal
- Use a spreadsheet
- Use a smartphone app or computer software that automatically downloads your banking data
- Use the spending tracker built into your mobile banking app

9. Save now for your children's education

The Taylors have done this right. They take full advantage of tax-assisted programs offered by the government to help save for their kid's post-secondary education. The government created the Registered Education Savings Plan (RESP) for this purpose. Although the amounts you put into an RESP are not tax-deductible — that is, you must first pay any tax due on the money you contribute — you don't pay tax on any gains or investment income you earn while the funds remain in the plan.

The other major benefit of saving money in an RESP is that the government will also contribute funds into the plan; their contribution is called a Canada Education Savings Grant. The amount of the grant is 20 percent of contributions to a maximum of $500 per child per year, with a lifetime limit of $7,200. See **Further Resources** at **robintaub.com** for additional resources related to RESPs.

Earnings accumulated in the RESP, as well as government grants, must be used to pay for the cost of post-secondary education. These amounts are taxable income to the student in the year paid out (they can use the tuition tax credit, plus other tax credits, to offset tax they'd otherwise owe). The original contributions can be paid out to the student or parent tax-free.

10. Present a united money front

It complicates matters when parents don't agree on important issues. This is especially true when it comes to money, which is why disagreement over money issues is one of the leading causes of divorce. But it's really important for parents to present a united money front. If your kids sense an opportunity to get what they want by exploiting the fact that their parents are not on the same page, they will take full advantage. As we've seen, values influence your financial behaviour, and it's best if you and your partner can arrive at shared values. In addition to showing your kids that it's possible to discuss and come to agreement about money, it also makes it much easier to set financial goals for your family.

11. Prepare a will and powers of attorney

The Taylors understood the importance of having a will that would reflect their wishes should something happen to them. When you die, everything you own and everything you owe go into a separate legal entity called your estate. If you have a will, it names an executor (or more than one) who is responsible for managing these assets and liabilities in your estate and making distributions to your beneficiaries (the people you've named in your will to receive an inheritance). An executor can be a trusted friend or family member who's willing and able to do the job, or a professional trustee.

Your will reflects how you want your estate to be distributed upon your death. It also names guardians for minor children, like Emma. However, when you die without a will (intestate), the distribution is decided by a formula laid down by the provincial government — not you — and this formula can vary from province to province. Wherever you live, the bottom line is that *your* wishes for how your property, possessions and personal effects are given away will not be considered.

The Taylors also prepared powers of attorney for both health and property. These documents authorize another person to act on your behalf on health and financial matters if you became mentally or physically incompetent and unable to act on your own behalf.

Managing finances responsibly can seem like a daunting task. Maybe you're already doing it well. If so, congratulations! If not, though, I hope some of the information and resources in this chapter will help you get your own financial matters in order. And the following chapters should help you talk about money management with your kids in a way that they can relate to at different stages of their young lives.

KEY POINTS

- The wisest investment you can make is in your kids. Kids who learn lessons about money management from a young age have a better chance of becoming healthy, happy, and successful adults who are financially responsible and independent.
- As a parent, you're a role model for your kids — probably their most important role model. This is just as true in money matters as in other important aspects of life. The best way to teach your kids to be money-smart is to be smart about money yourself and to talk to them about how money works.
- Eleven Healthy Habits of Financial Management:

  1. Know where you stand financially
  2. Live within your means
  3. Save, or pay yourself first
  4. Understand the difference between good debt and bad debt
  5. Set up a financial safety net
  6. Know the difference between needs and wants

7. Teach delayed gratification and set financial goals
8. Track your spending
9. Save now for your children's education
10. Present a united money front
11. Prepare a will and powers of attorney

RESOURCES

Role Model Self-Assessment[5]

Answer these statements with either True or False

	True or False
I wouldn't stretch myself financially in order to drive a nice car.	
I try to stay up-to-date on the tax issues that affect me.	
I like to discuss investments.	
If I won the lottery, I wouldn't noticeably change my lifestyle.	
I'm usually eager to get to work.	
Learning is an important key to financial success.	
I'm reasonably careful with money.	
I adhere to a structured budget.	
I always conduct due diligence on my investments.	
When I get advice, I seek a second opinion.	
I keep well informed for everyday financial decisions.	
I know where I'm going and how to get there.	

5. Inspired by Financial Attitudes Exercise in *Client–Centred Life Planning* by Michael R. Curtis (Toronto, Canada: Michael R. Curtis, 2005).

	True or False
If there is something I want but don't need, I walk away and sleep on it.	
I pay off my credit card balance every month.	
I reflect on my past investment decisions to see what I can learn.	
I don't gamble with my savings by taking excess risks.	
I try to shop carefully, using coupons and waiting for sales.	
I can afford everything I need.	

Fewer than 10 Trues: You have some work to do!

10–15 Trues: You're modelling good behaviour some of the time. Keep working on it!

15–18 Trues: Congratulations, you're modelling good behaviour almost all the time!

Cash Flow Calculator

CREATE A BUDGET

Use this tool to help give you a clear picture of your cash flow.

Monthly Income	
Salary after taxes (take-home pay, self-employment/business income)	$
Other income (e.g., investment income)	$
Total Income	$
Monthly Expenses — Fixed	
Housing costs (e.g., mortgage, rent, condo/maintenance fees, property taxes, etc.)	$
Utilities — heat, hydro, water	$
Services — phone, cable/satellite, internet, security system	$
Insurance — auto, home, life, disability	$
Child care	$
Existing loans and credit cards (minimum monthly payments)	$
Other fixed expenses (e.g., child support, alimony, etc.)	$
Total Expenses — Fixed	$
Monthly Expenses — Variable	
Groceries	$
Household maintenance (e.g., renovations, landscaping and gardening, housecleaning, snow removal, lawn care, etc.)	$

Transportation (e.g., car lease, gas, transit, car service and repairs, parking fees, licence and registration, etc.)	$
Uninsured health services (e.g., prescriptions, dental care, eye care, counselling, any other health services not covered under a plan)	$
Education (e.g., tuition, books, exam fees, etc.)	$
Long-term savings (e.g., monthly pension plan, RSP, education saving contribution)	$
Other variable expenses	$
Total Expenses — Variable	$
Monthly Expenses — Discretionary	
Personal (e.g., clothing, shoes, gifts, salon, gym membership, etc.)	$
Daily living (e.g., pet expenses, dry cleaning, etc.)	$
Entertainment (e.g., streaming services, takeout and delivery, dining out, movies (in-theatre and on-demand), music, theatre/concerts, etc.)	$
Donations	$
Vacation	$
Other discretionary expenses	$
Total Expenses — Discretionary	$
Monthly Cash Flow	
Total Income	$
Total Expenses (Fixed, Variable and Discretionary)	$
Net Cash Flow (Total Income minus Total Expenses)	$

Net Worth Worksheet

ASSETS AND LIABILITIES

Use this handy financial worksheet for a snapshot of what you own (your assets) and what you owe (your liabilities). Record the value of all assets and liabilities, putting a realistic market value on tangible assets such as property, car(s), etc.

Assets and Liabilities	
Assets (What You Own)	
Non-registered assets	
Chequing/savings account(s)	$
GICs/term deposits	$
Canada Savings Bonds	$
Stocks, bonds, mutual funds	$
Investment properties	$
Cash value of life insurance	$
Home(s)	$
Automobile(s)	$
Boat(s)	$
Subtotal: non-registered assets	$
Registered assets	
RRSPs, TFSAs, RESPs, DPSPs, RRIFs	$
Locked-in RRSPs, LIRAs, LIFs, LRIFs	$
Value of pension plan(s)	$
Other (e.g., annuities)	$
Subtotal: registered assets	$
Total Assets (non-registered plus registered)	$

Liabilities (What You Owe)	
Mortgage(s)[6]	$
Income/property taxes owing	$
Car loan/lease[7]	$
Credit card balance(s)	$
Personal line of credit	$
Other loans	$
Other debts	$
Unpaid bills	$
Other obligations[8]	$
Total Liabilities	$

NET WORTH

Assets and Liabilities	
Total Assets	$
Total Liabilities	($)
Net Worth (Total Assets minus Total Liabilities)	$

---

6. Outstanding principal on mortgage(s).

7. Outstanding principal on car loan or total outstanding lease obligation.

8. Annual amount of other obligations including daycare, alimony payments, etc.

Values Validator[9]

HELPING YOU DISCOVER WHAT IS REALLY IMPORTANT TO YOU

Use this method of ranking:

Not important	0
Somewhat important	1–3
Quite important	4–7
Very important	8–10

	Value	Description	Rating (out of 10)
1	Academics	I have a high regard for scholastic pursuits	
2	Achievement	It's important to accomplish my goals	
3	Activity	I like to be fully occupied at all times	
4	Advancement	I want the opportunity for career advancement	
5	Adventure	I like to do things in new and interesting ways	
6	Enjoyment	I want to enjoy life and have fun	
7	Expertise	I want to be a known authority in my field	

9. Adapted from Values worksheet in Financial Attitudes Exercise in *Client-Centred Life Planning* by Michael R. Curtis (Toronto, Canada: Michael R. Curtis, 2005).

8	Family	I want to contribute to family members	
9	Friendship	I want close companionship	
10	Health	I want to be healthy and pursue a healthy lifestyle	
11	Independence	I like to be able to work or do things alone and free from constraints	
12	Location	I want to be able to live anywhere	
13	Power	I want to have influence over my future	
14	Prestige	I like to obtain recognition and status	
15	Routine	I like to have a set daily schedule	
16	Security	I like to minimize adverse changes in my life	
17	Self-Development	I want to be the best that I can be	
18	Self-Realization	I like to realize the full potential of my skills and abilities	
19	Social Service	I want to serve others	
20	Wealth	I want to be able to afford opportunities	

Rank your top five values:

_____

_____

_____

_____

_____

CHAPTER 2

Teaching Young Children

A Roadmap for Children Five to Eight

Years Old

Normally, kids become familiar with money at a very early age because they see us use it daily. In most families, teaching kids about money begins when they start asking about it and when they start asking for things! This usually begins to happen around the time a child starts preschool or elementary school. For instance, your kid may see the toys, books, and clothing that other kids have and begin asking for specific items or even brands. Even if we're using cash less often than we used to, your child may still express curiosity about money when they do see it: the way it looks, the different colours on our paper bills, and the different sizes and shapes of the coins we use.

"At about age five to seven they ask for things. We teach them that nothing comes for free."

Earn

WHAT IS MONEY?

BILLS AND COINS

How do you teach young kids about money in an increasingly cash-free world? The answer, especially with younger kids, still starts with cash. It's tactile, concrete (not abstract), and engaging. Handing cash to somebody feels very real, a sense of loss that is hard to replicate with plastic or your phone.

At this age, if you're comfortable letting your kids handle money (after sanitizing, perhaps) they can start to develop an understanding of Canadian currency. Even though we're using cash less and less, it's still prudent to have some cash on hand in case of emergency. You can show them the different coins and bills and talk to them about what they're worth. You can point out the different images on the "heads" and "tails" sides of the coins and discuss how each of them is a very special and important image of Canada: the beaver, the moose, the loon, and the polar bear, to name a few. Point out the different dates on each coin and see if your kids can find a coin from the year they were born. You can also tell your kids that our coins are made by the Royal Canadian Mint (www.mint.ca) and discuss what metals the coins are made of:

- nickels, dimes and quarters: steel, copper, and nickel
- loonies: brass-plated steel
- toonies: bronze

In addition to everyday coins, show them special coins like fifty-cent pieces and silver dollars or commemorative coins like the Terry Fox loonie or the poppy quarter. There are even pure silver glow-in-the-dark coins!

There are lots of facts about money that your kids may find interesting at this age and as they get older. Our colourful polymer bills are printed by the Bank of Canada and have special markings and security features like raised ink, metallic portraits, and transparent images to prevent people from making counterfeit money.

Discussing who appears on the bills and coins can also be a history (not just a math) lesson! You can check out the Bank of Canada website for other money matters that might intrigue your kids: www.bankofcanada.

ca/banknotes. And if your kids are really interested in money, you may want to visit the currency museum website, especially the resources in the Learning Centre at www.bankofcanadamuseum.ca.

Generally, young children are able to count to ten and have a basic knowledge of numbers and quantities. To teach them what money is worth, you can make it fun by playing games.

THINGS TO DO

Games with coins

Help your kid sort a jar of coins into different piles:

- Show her a nickel and explain that a nickel is worth five cents.
- Ask her to pick up an additional nickel and exchange the nickels for one dime; explain that a dime is worth ten cents, twice as much as a nickel.
- Give her a quarter, explaining that it's worth 25 cents and is more valuable than a nickel or a dime.

As she gets older, the games can become a bit more challenging:

- Ask her what combination of nickels and dimes she'd have to give in exchange for a quarter.
- Move on to the loonie and the toonie, which

> will be especially appealing to her because
> of their size, shape, and colour (and their
> relative value).
> - Describe the loonie as being worth 100
>   cents or one dollar and challenge your kid
>   to find different combinations of nickels,
>   dimes, or quarters that would add up to one
>   loonie.
> - Ask if she can guess what the toonie is
>   worth, based on the sound of its name!

BARTER

Your kids may be curious about why we use money to buy
things. They may ask you how bills and coins became the
way to pay for things. If your kids are at the upper end of
the age range, you may want to start by explaining that
money replaced the barter system. Centuries ago, it was
much harder for people to get what they needed. Instead
of using coins and currency, all they had to offer as payment was goods or services in exchange for whatever the
other person had. This is called "barter." For example, if
you were a grape grower, you could exchange your grapes
for the potato farmer's potatoes. Or you could hire workers to help you with the harvest and pay them in grapes.
But because grapes were all you had to exchange, if you
needed a chicken and the chicken farmer didn't want or
need grapes, you would not be able to get any chicken. As
a result, most societies realized that they needed something that everyone agreed had value and could be used

to pay for things — money.

In the earliest days, money was made out of whatever was rare or highly desired, like beads, whale teeth, feathers, and even huge stone discs carved out of limestone! Slowly, almost every country switched to a much more convenient system of bills and coins backed by the government.

FAMILY DISCUSSION

Foreign currency

Explain to your kids that other countries don't have the same money as us and that if you travel to another country, you cannot use your Canadian money. You have to exchange Canadian money for the local currency. Not all countries use dollars — some use yen or euros. And just because another country's bill says $1, it doesn't mean that it's worth the same as our $1 coin! We may have to pay more than $1, say $1.20, to buy a single unit of another currency.

FOREIGN CURRENCIES

Your kids may be interested in currency from other countries because it looks so different from Canadian money. For example, you may want to show your child an American $1 or $5 bill. Unlike our bills, American bills are all a similar green colour and so they're a little harder to tell apart. Also, coins from foreign countries can be interesting to young kids, especially ones that have holes in the centre and ones that are made from different materials and feel different from our coins.

DIGITAL MONEY

Young kids aren't ready or able to grasp the concept of digital money. But as they get older, you can begin to introduce debit and credit cards and show them how to pay with plastic. From there, you can move on to digital tools like apps.

THE VALUE OF A DOLLAR

Every parent says they want their kids to know and appreciate the value of a dollar. But young kids are not very worldly, so it's harder for them to appreciate what things cost. The challenge is to explain relative value by using examples they can relate to, like toys or food. You can show them that one apple costs one loonie but one ice cream cone costs three loonies, so an ice cream cone is worth three times as much (or is three times as expensive) as an apple. If a toy that they want costs $20, you can show them that you'd have to pay for it with 20 loonies, which means it's worth 20 times more than an apple and nearly seven times more than an ice cream cone. We will discuss more opportunities to teach young kids the value of a dollar later in this chapter under **Teachable Moments.**

"We started with coins. What does a quarter buy? Four quarters equals one dollar; what does one dollar buy? You can teach what things cost this way and go on to percents and interest and return on investment."

WHERE DOES MONEY COME FROM? (NO, THE ANSWER ISN'T THE ATM!)

"When I tell my seven-year-old daughter that I don't have any more money for toys or candy, she tells me to go to the ATM!"

It's funny, but it also reminds us that young kids may not always understand where money comes from. They may think it actually does grow on trees or come from a magic machine that spits out bills. They're probably too young to appreciate what making a living is all about and how hard you have to work to earn money. But they can understand that you work, doing whatever it is you do, in order to make money for the family.

You can explain to them that the money you make gets deposited into your bank account, which is connected to the bank machine. The money you withdraw pays for food, clothes, the car — all the things at home that they can see and touch. It also pays for some things they can't see, like the mortgage on the house or rent on the apartment where you live, heat and air conditioning, electricity, and the internet. You can also explain that you're able to buy them things they want, like toys or candy, in addition to things they need, and what the difference is. They're not too young to be grateful for what they have and to know that there are others who are less fortunate.

FAMILY DISCUSSION

Jobs

- Ask your kids to name some other jobs they see people do, e.g., teacher, dentist, eye doctor, garbage collector, or mail carrier.
- Ask them what kind of education they might need to do that job. Discuss the connection between education, jobs/careers, and making money.

"My son understands that you need to work to earn money to live. He's aware of the fact that his mom and dad work in order to buy him his favourite food or toy. He often says to me that he wants to work on his computer to make money, because he sees his mom and dad working on their computers. It's never too early to start. He even pretends to use a plastic card as his credit card!"

If you take your young kids with you the next time you make a deposit or a withdrawal, tell them to think of the ATM as a giant piggy bank: you can put money in or take money out. But if you don't make any money, you have nothing to deposit, and the bank card will be useless because there is no money to withdraw. You may also consider showing your child your online bank statement; the money you deposit is added to your account, and the money you withdraw is deducted. When you punch in your PIN, explain that this secret code makes sure that only you can deposit or withdraw money to and from your account and that it must be kept secret.

BIRTHDAY AND TOOTH FAIRY MONEY

There are special occasions when young kids "earn" or receive money. Your kids may get money from the tooth fairy when they lose their baby teeth and/or money from friends and family on their birthdays or on significant holidays or milestones. These are important opportunities to introduce them to the concept that when you earn money, you have choices: save, spend, share, and invest. It's important to choose well, because once the money is spent, it's no longer available for other things.

"My son was saving up to buy Squishies, those cute, cuddly, squishy toys that were the hottest fad. When he finally had enough money, he ran to the store, bought the Squishies, and headed straight to his friend's house to play. But his friend, and all the other kids, had already moved on to the next fad and were no longer interested in Squishies. Suddenly, neither was my son. He no longer had any money, but he learned two important lessons: when it's gone, it's gone, and don't fall for every fad!"

ALLOWANCE: PAYMENT FOR CHORES, A MONEY MANAGEMENT TOOL, OR BOTH?

Allowance has become a controversial topic among parents and financial experts. But it never used to be. When

I was growing up, you got an allowance for doing some basic chores around the house. If you didn't do them, your parents held back your allowance. Back then, no one thought of allowance as a money management tool. Parents didn't consider that by withholding their kid's allowance, they were depriving them of the opportunity to learn how to manage money when the stakes were low.

Some parents firmly believe that their kids need to "earn" their allowance, perhaps by doing household chores or getting good grades (more on that in Chapter 3). They believe that this establishes a connection between putting forth an effort and earning money. Others believe just as strongly that their kids should help out around the house without getting paid because it's their responsibility as a member of the family to contribute. They believe that paying them sends the wrong message, i.e., that they should expect compensation for everything they do. There is no right or wrong answer. As always, you have to do what works for your child and your family.

FAMILY DISCUSSION

Allowance

What is your philosophy about allowance?

- Payment for chores
- Payment for good grades
- A money management tool

WHEN DO I START AND HOW MUCH DO I GIVE?

For young kids, one rule of thumb is to base their allowance on their age. For example, a five-year-old could get $5 a week and a seven-year-old could get $7. It's simple and makes sense to kids. Another strategy is to estimate what your child reasonably spends in a week (say $3 on treats) and then add a little more for savings, sharing, and investing. You also have to decide what's affordable for your family. Pay allowance on a regular basis so that it feels like a steady income your kids can rely on.

LIMITATIONS OR LAISSEZ-FAIRE?

Because of their age and level of maturity, young children need more guidance when it comes to money choices than older children. Although they may already be consumers, at this age they don't have a realistic attitude about money. As the marshmallow test in Chapter 1 taught us, some have not yet developed self-discipline and impulse control. They need training, and they respond well to a parent or teacher who is willing to teach financial concepts in a fun way.

Save

In Chapter 1 we talked about the importance of delayed gratification, setting goals, and saving. Saving is basically deferred spending. When it comes to saving, almost any toy or item your child wants can become a goal. The next time your child asks for a certain toy or game, suggest that he use his allowance to save for it. Once enough money has been saved up, take him to the store to make the big purchase or order it together online!

"I was once at a toy store and there was a woman ahead of me in line with her young son. He had his little toys on the counter and was counting out his money to pay for them. But he came up short — by only $2. I could see how disappointed he was, and I was tempted to just hand him a toonie. But then I looked over at his mother, and I could see that she was standing her ground — that she was trying to teach him something. He chose one toy and put it back. He didn't have the money to pay for it, and this was the lesson his mother was trying to teach him."

Although the woman taught her son a valuable lesson, you have to be careful not to discourage your kids from reaching their goals, especially if it's their first attempt at saving. One way to effectively encourage your kids toward a goal is to offer to match their savings. If your child agrees to save $5 toward a

$10 toy, you can offer to match their savings with an additional $5.

MULTI-SLOTTED PIGGY BANKS

Piggy banks are an old-fashioned way to teach young kids to save and are still popular today.

But piggy banks have come a long way — we now have multi-slotted piggy banks. They have a built-in feature to help young kids make smart and deliberate money choices: separate slots and compartments for save, spend, share, and invest!

Using their allowance, birthday money, or tooth fairy money, your child can decide how much to allocate to each category. Remember to give them their allowance in different denominations to make it easier for them to make the allocations. (See www.moneysavvy.com)

"I like the kind of piggy bank that you can't open, that you literally have to break open with a hammer when it gets full. Otherwise, if you can open it, it's too tempting to borrow or steal from your savings, and the next thing you know, the piggy bank is empty!"

"We started with a piggy bank (actually an empty hot chocolate container, which the kids decorated themselves) and when they had accumulated $50, we moved that money to a bank account."

Spend

TEACHABLE MOMENTS

Since young kids are often with you when they're out in the world, opportunities will arise to teach them about money. You don't have to set aside extra time. These opportunities will occur organically in your everyday lives. Think of them as teachable moments.

You have a lot of influence over your kids at this age. Although they're also influenced by siblings, peers, and both traditional and social media, they place the most confidence in what you, their parents, say. And you know what's appropriate for your own kids, so take advantage of situations as they arise to teach them to make smart choices.

AT THE GROCERY STORE, CORNER STORE AND MALL

Every transaction, whether at the store or at your computer, is a chance to teach your kids about money. At a store, when the cashier gives you your total, and if the store still accepts cash, ask your child to help you count out the money you owe. Then have her pay for the items and count the change she gets back, making sure it's the right amount. Teach her to get a receipt, in case a mistake is made and you have to return something.

Many stores have added self-checkout, and your kids may find it fun to help you scan the items you're buying. If you pay with your debit card, show your kids that it's the same card you use to deposit and withdraw money at the ATM. Explain that using a bank card in a store means that the cost of whatever you buy comes out of your bank account right away. Show them that for amounts above $100, you punch in the same secret code at the store that you used at the ATM. Remind them that the secret code means that only you can buy things and pay for them with the money in your account. For amounts below $100, you can show them that all you have to do is "tap" your card.

AT A RESTAURANT

Next time you take your kids out to dinner (or pick up takeout) and you pay using your credit card, take the time to teach them what a credit card is and how it works. Explain to them that, unlike paying with cash or your debit card, when you pay with your credit card the money doesn't come out of your bank account right away. Instead, you're allowed to pay later, when the credit card bill is due.

PLANNING A BIRTHDAY PARTY

Before the coronavirus pandemic hit, children's birthdays provided opportunities to teach valuable money lessons, as we will see here and under **Share** below. Involving your kids in planning their birthday parties can introduce them to the idea of budgeting in a fun way. (However, birthday parties may be a little different in a world of social distancing, mask wearing and limits on gatherings.)

For Emma Taylor's eighth birthday, she really wanted to have a movie party. The latest Disney movie had just come out, and she and all her friends couldn't wait to see it. She spoke to her parents about the idea, and they said yes, as long as Emma agreed to help plan it. Michelle and Robert realized that planning the party could be a teachable moment. They sat down with Emma to talk about all the different costs: the cost of a child's movie ticket, the cost of a few adult movie tickets (for the chaperones), the cost of snacks like popcorn, candy, and drinks, and the cost of an ice cream cake for the party after.

Emma wanted to use e-vites to save money and paper. They settled on an overall budget for the party, and Robert explained to Emma that the more kids she invited, the more the party would cost. So Emma thought really hard and invited only her close friends in order to keep the cost of the party within her budget.

GAMES AND APPS

Board games have always been popular, but now apps, especially games that teach money lessons, are also catching on.

In the Taylor house, they love playing games like Monopoly, where the object of the game is to become the wealthiest player through buying, renting, and selling property. They also like playing the game of Life. This game simulates a person's travels through his or her life, from college to retirement, with jobs, marriages, and possibly children along the way.

You can now buy digital versions of these classic games. For example, Monopoly has electronic banking instead of paper, which lets players collect rent, buy properties, and pay fines with the touch of a button.

Life also comes with interactive digital content, but be warned — there are in-app purchases that can add up quickly!

There are also money apps that are suitable for young children. See **Further Resources** at **robintaub.com** for some examples.

Share

GET A GIFT/GIVE A GIFT

Birthday parties are a really big deal for young kids. It's something they look forward to all year — having fun with their friends, eating cake, and getting presents!

On Emma Taylor's seventh birthday, Robert and Michelle let her invite all the kids in her class to her party, but they really didn't think Emma needed 20 gifts. They felt that her birthday could be an opportunity to teach her about sharing and decided to use Echoage. com. Echoage is a website that lets you collect funds from guests that are then split between a charity of your choice and a group gift. The website also helps you send out party invitations, collect RSVPs, and send thank you notes. Emma chose World Wildlife Fund (WWF) from a list of charities that support many different causes, such as kids, health, animals, camps, relief, the earth, and schools, to name a few. She also got one very special gift that had been on her birthday wish list. Emma was really excited to receive the gift she had been wanting for so long, but she was also really happy that some of her gifts went to WWF. The Taylors were also happy for Emma to have a tangible example of delayed gratification: the special birthday gift that had been on her wish list all year.

DONATING TO CHARITY — IT ADDS UP!

Michelle Taylor remembers a trip to Shopper's Drug Mart with Emma to pick up a prescription, when the cashier asked them if they wanted to add a dollar or two to their total, to donate to charity. Emma started to think about all of the customers that came in and out of that one store all day long. And she started to think about how if everyone donated just a dollar or two, it could really add up.

Invest

ENCOURAGING ENTREPRENEURSHIP — BEYOND THE LEMONADE STAND

Emma Taylor was always very enterprising, even as a young kid. When all the other little kids on her street set up lemonade stands, Emma decided she wanted to do something just a little bit different. She had always enjoyed art at school and even took an extracurricular art program at a local art school. She was quite prolific — all the different pieces she had created were really starting to accumulate. So Emma decided to create an art gallery in her parents' backyard to showcase her art. She invited all of her friends, their parents, her family, and her neighbours to view and buy pieces of her art. She priced each piece based on the amount of time it had taken her to create it and what she thought people would pay for it, making sure she covered the cost of her supplies. She sent out e-vites and bought some refreshments to serve during the show.

The show was a big success! Many "art patrons" bought pieces of Emma's art, and with each sale Emma recorded the name of the piece and the amount it had sold for in a notebook. She also made sure to give each customer a receipt.

At the end of the show, Emma added up all the sales she had recorded in her notebook to determine her gross sales. Then she deducted the costs, including the refreshments she had served.

Emma turned a nice profit! She paid herself first by allocating some to savings, set aside some proceeds for donating and spending, and invested the rest — on more art supplies for her growing business!

KEY POINTS

- Kids are curious. They spend a lot of time just trying to figure out how the world works. If they're old enough to ask questions about money, then they're old enough to deserve a good answer.

- You don't have to schedule a family conference to have great conversations with your kid about money. Opportunities will present themselves countless times in your everyday life. The trick is to recognize those "teachable moments" and to take advantage of them.

- Teaching kids about money can be fun for them and for you. Capitalize on this fun factor when you talk to your kid about money—education can have a big element of entertainment at this age.

CHAPTER 3

Teaching Preteens

A Roadmap for Preteens Nine to

Twelve Years Old

As your kids become a little older, you will be noticing many changes. Hopefully they're a little more responsible and mature, and certainly at this age they have a better grasp of math. Perhaps they're more interested in money now than when they were younger. But just like younger kids, preteens have money choices, and as parents it's your job to give them the right tools and knowledge to make sensible ones.

Earn

JOBS: BABYSITTING, TUTORING AND OTHER ODD JOBS

Because your preteen is also a little more independent, they have the opportunity to earn money by working "odd jobs." A job can make them more responsible. For many preteens, their first job is babysitting. Schools often offer babysitting training and "certification" for kids in Grade 6 or 7. However, physical distancing measures in place during the pandemic may mean fewer parents needing or feeling comfortable with babysitters outside of the family. So encourage your kids to babysit for immediate or extended family. As things return to the "new normal", they can expand to friends or neighbours.

"When I was around 11, I loved babysitting my neighbours' three kids. I didn't really have a social life yet, so I didn't feel like I was missing anything if I babysat on the weekend. The kids were usually well behaved and went to bed early. I would play games with them, maybe watch a movie, and read them a story before bedtime. Sometimes the oldest boy would stay up with me to watch the hockey game. We lived right across

the street, so I knew I could call my mom to help me if there was a problem. And they always had the best snacks! Looking back, it was probably the easiest money I ever made."

Other jobs that are suitable for your preteen include shovelling snow, washing cars, or cutting grass. Encourage them to be creative when looking to make extra money. If they're technically inclined, perhaps they can tutor an adult on computer or social media use (sometimes referred to as "reverse mentoring"). Or, if they're strong academically, maybe they can tutor younger students in reading or math. Some of this may take place remotely.

These jobs are likely to pay differently. The going rate for an hour of babysitting may be less than they can make washing a car for an hour. If your preteen is trying to save up for something specific in a very short period of time, he may look for the job with the highest pay.

At this age, if they like what they're doing they're more likely to stick with it. They will get to experience the satisfaction of doing something they enjoy and doing it well — and getting paid for it! As they get older and start thinking about career choices, this will be an important message: when you're passionate about what you do, it doesn't feel like "work."

ALLOWANCE REVISITED: PAYMENT FOR CHORES, A MONEY MANAGEMENT TOOL, OR BOTH?

As highlighted in Chapter 2, different parents have different philosophies about allowance. Some see it as payment for chores, some see it as a way to teach their kids money management skills, and some see it as both. Usually when kids are in their preteen years their allowance increases, and therefore the stakes get higher about how they use it. What's important is that you're clear with your kid about what your philosophy is and that your kid understands why she's getting an allowance, why it's the amount it is, and what her responsibilities are regarding how the money will be used.

KNOW WHAT MOTIVATES YOUR KID

What motivates your preteen? Is she motivated by extrinsic rewards like money? (There's nothing wrong with that — we're all motivated to varying degrees by money.) If that's the case, paying her to do her assigned chores will ensure they get done and will give her some money to manage. But if she doesn't do her chores, do you take away her allowance? Often, as parents, we do this as a knee-jerk reaction because it feels like the only leverage we have. But we're probably better off letting our kids get their allowance so they can continue to practise managing money. There are plenty of other consequences that can be meted out for not doing chores — like less time on the computer, phone, or Xbox!

"When my daughter doesn't do her chores, rather than take away her allowance, I take away access to the computer, her phone, and video games — things I don't want her spending so much time on anyway!"

But maybe your kid is intrinsically motivated. Does he have the drive and discipline to do his chores or his homework without connecting it to his allowance? If that's the case, then his allowance can be given as a pure money management tool.

Finally, you can always give your kids opportunities to earn extra money by doing things around the house that go above and beyond their normal responsibilities.

"My kids were always looking for opportunities to earn a little extra money. So I told them that if I had to hire and pay someone to do something, like mow the lawn, shovel snow, or rake leaves, then I would be happy to pay them instead. But taking out the garbage did not count — I certainly wasn't going to hire anyone outside the family to do that!"

HOW MUCH ALLOWANCE TO GIVE?

The age formula that you used to decide how much allowance to give when your kids were younger is probably no longer appropriate. At this stage, their allowance should be based on a budget.

"When my son turned 11, he asked for a raise in his allowance. I told him that if he wanted to get more money, he had to take a course about money that his school was offering as an after-school program. To my amazement, he agreed!"

HOW TO GIVE ALLOWANCE

Should you still use cash to pay your preteens an allowance? Many parents don't often use cash or have it handy on allowance day. That's where digital payments and apps come in. You may find that not only are they more convenient for you, but they also teach your kids about money. For examples of apps you could use, please see **Further Resources** at **robintaub.com.** Although apps can be great tools, they're no substitute for parental guidance and ongoing discussions with your kids about money.

LIMITATIONS OR LAISSEZ-FAIRE

Once your child receives his allowance, try to resist the urge to get overly involved in what he does with it. Explain that he should allocate his allowance to the different categories of save, spend, share, and invest. You can be somewhat hands-off, as his spending should be guided by the budget you created together. Allow him to make his own spending choices and to live with the consequences of his own decisions. However, it's still a good idea to sit down regularly and see if he's managing to stay within budget.

The budget may need tweaking if you've under- or overestimated his spending. Also, debriefing after a big purchase or a money mistake is always valuable. We'll discuss this later in this chapter.

"The hardest thing I've had to do as a parent is let my kids fail at something and face the consequences. It's no different with money. They need the freedom to make mistakes and learn from the consequences. I don't rescue them, but I also don't say 'I told you so.' I don't always make the right financial decisions either, so it's important for them to see that we all learn from our mistakes."

FAMILY DISCUSSION

Allowance

- Sit down with your preteen and review what their typical week looks like: when, where, and how they're likely to need money and how much is reasonable.
- This is money they're going to spend anyway, so use their allowance to start shifting some of the responsibility to them.
- Making the budgeting process collaborative will give your preteen a sense of empowerment and control over their spending. It will also result in buy-in.

Save

PIGGY BANKS TO REAL BANKS

Around this age, your kid is ready to graduate from a piggy bank to a bank account. The advantages of a bank account include the opportunity to earn interest on their savings as well as the security of having their money in a safe place. If you bring your child with you to a brick and mortar branch to open their first account, try to do most of the paperwork with the bank ahead of time. Sometimes these processes take longer than you expect, and you don't want your kid to get bored and lose interest — this should be an exciting day! Another option to consider is a digital or online-only bank, where the entire account opening process is done on a computer or phone.

Some kids may resist because it feels like they're losing their money. So show them their bank balance and how it keeps growing every time they empty their piggy bank (or their savings compartment) to make a deposit. That should encourage them!

Youth accounts are special accounts designed for young savers. While generally there are no fees, they also pay very low rates of interest, which makes this the perfect time to discuss the concept of interest with your preteen: the bank is paying them to keep their savings there. You may also want to add that if you have to borrow money from the bank, they will charge you interest for using their money.

Let your kid know that the bank card they get with their account can be a convenient way to make withdrawals and to check their balance online. (More about debit cards below.) With a youth account, often withdrawals are limited by the bank; for example, up to $20 or $25 per week. Your preteen will be responsible for creating and protecting their own PIN, but you may want to reinforce the importance of not telling anyone what their PIN is, not even their closest friends.

MATCHING SAVINGS

An effective way to encourage preteens to save toward a goal they've chosen is to offer to match their savings. In fact, you may even have experienced matched savings yourself if you work for a company that matches retirement or other savings. Also, if you have contributed to an RESP for your child, the government gives grants of 20 percent of contributions made to an RESP (up to $500 per beneficiary per year). For the recipient, this is like getting free money, and most rational people would take full advantage!

FAMILY DISCUSSION

ATM use

- Do you think your preteen is ready to make unsupervised ATM or bank branch deposits or withdrawals? What about making online purchases using their virtual debit card?
- Do you trust them to keep their own bank card and to safeguard their PIN?

CHEQUING ACCOUNTS

While on the topic of bank accounts, you can talk to your preteen about how you use a chequing account. Explain that writing a cheque is one way to pay someone; it is often more convenient than using cash and also more secure. Only the person to whom the cheque is written can cash it and, unlike cash, if a cheque is lost or stolen you can stop payment on it. Cheques are certainly preferred when you have to mail a payment or pay a plumber who makes a service call, but hardly anyone uses personal cheques anymore.

Electronic transfers (e-transfers) are an even more convenient way to send, request, or receive money directly from one bank account to another. With Interac e-Transfer, all you need is access to online or mobile banking through your financial institution and you can send money to or request money from anyone with an email address or mobile phone number and a bank account in Canada — without sharing any personal financial information.

THINGS TO DO

Chequing accounts

- Show your preteen how you keep track of the money in your chequing account by recording every cheque you write as well as other additions to and withdrawals from the account, such as automatic bill payments and e-transfers.

- By balancing your cheque book (reconciling it to your bank balance), you're modelling financial responsibility for your child.
- You're demonstrating the importance of keeping track of your money, knowing if you have enough to cover any cheques you write or withdrawals you make.
- You can explain that if you "bounce" a cheque, the bank charges a big fee and the recipient doesn't get paid.
- Explain that managing your bank accounts and paying bills online is extremely efficient and convenient.

A STORY ABOUT SETTING GOALS

Emma Taylor and her best friend, Allison, really wanted new headphones. When Allison asked her mom to buy her new headphones, her mom told her to start saving her birthday and holiday money. She also recommended that Allison save some of her allowance or do some extra work around the house to earn even more money. At first, Allison worked really hard to earn extra income and was really disciplined about putting her savings in her piggy bank. She was well on her way to saving enough for new headphones.

One day, when Allison was out with her friends, she told them how much money she had in her piggy bank. Her friends begged her to buy them ice cream. Allison wanted to be generous to her friends, so she took some money out of her piggy bank to treat her friends. Next, they wanted to go to the movies, and they wanted Allison to pay, since she had so much money. She didn't know how to say no, so she took some more money from her piggy bank. She also sponsored one of her friends in a charity walk. Every day, Allison kept finding more and more interesting things to spend her money on. But she wasn't saving for new headphones anymore. When she spent her money on other things, she gave up saving for new headphones.

Emma planned differently. She earned income from doing extra chores around the house. She used her multi-slotted piggy bank to save most of her allowance and birthday money, but set a little aside for spending today and some for sharing with others. When Emma's friends begged her to buy them ice cream, candy, or movie tickets, she'd tell them that she was saving for new headphones, but she'd always remember to buy her friends a special treat on their birthdays. Before too long, Emma had saved enough money to buy new headphones.

Emma and Allison met at the mall so Emma could buy her new headphones. When they got there, Emma could see that Allison was really upset. Allison had spent all her money, and now she couldn't buy the one thing she really wanted — new headphones. Emma felt bad for Allison, but she was also happy that she had stuck to her plan and achieved her goal. She not only had enough money for new headphones, she also had a little left over for a pizza, which she shared with Allison to cheer her up.

Spend

GETTING OUT IN THE WORLD

Today's kids are becoming consumers at an earlier age than kids in the past. By the time they turn 12, they're making a lot of financial decisions on their own. Because our society places a lot of emphasis on consumption, and with the added pressures of social media, it can be hard for preteens to resist the desire to buy things. At this age, they spend money quickly and impulsively. Between the ages of 9 and 12, kids will develop consumption habits that stay with them for the rest of their lives. But they will also learn a lot from the mistakes they make — if you let them.

SPENDING THEIR OWN MONEY VERSUS YOURS

As we discussed earlier, giving your kids an allowance is one way to transfer some of the responsibility to them while also helping to reduce requests for money. When kids are spending their own money (even if you give it to them as allowance), they tend to think a lot longer and harder about a potential purchase, whether they really need it or just want it. "It's not worth that much, I don't want it" is something kids say when they have to spend their own money. When they're spending your money, it doesn't seem to "count" in the same way, and there is often less deliberation. Decide who pays for what and what comes out of their allowance by referring back to the budget you created together.

"My 12-year old brother is much younger than me — 18 years younger — so I often feel like a parent as much as a sister. When I take him to the mall, I remind him to bring his own money, in case he wants to buy something. As we walk through the food court, he always insists he doesn't want anything, he's not hungry — unless some-one else offers to pay!"

MEDIA AND ADVERTISING

Preteens are exposed to a lot of advertising, through the internet, TV, product placement, and especially social media. They're also exposed to advertising in public places, like public washrooms, taxis, public transit, and outdoor billboards. Even though they can distinguish between con-tent on YouTube and a commercial, they don't necessarily understand that the purpose of the commercial is to seduce you into buying things you wouldn't otherwise purchase.

"I try to explain to my preteen son that commer-cials and ads are designed to make him think that he needs a certain toy or pair of shoes in order to be happy, when really he just wants them because they're cool. I try to get him to think critically

about the ads he's seeing. I point out how they exaggerate the benefits of their products and downplay the negative features, and we laugh about catchphrases like 'healthy-looking skin' (shouldn't it be 'healthy skin'?)."

FAMILY DISCUSSION

Debrief purchases

When your kids save up to buy something with their own money, make the time to debrief afterwards with the following questions:

- Did they think it was worth the money?
- Was it worth the effort involved in earning it and saving for it? How many hours did they have to work to be able to buy it?
- What did they like or dislike about the shopping experience?
- What, if anything, would they do differently next time?

SOCIAL MEDIA AND PEER PRESSURE

Even though you still have primary influence over your preteen's spending, at this age they rely heavily on what their friends think. By age 12, most kids will side with their peers over their parents when it comes to purchasing decisions. This has been amplified by social media, where they're bombarded with images of what others have and do. They recognize brands and like to have the latest clothes, shoes, or cell phones and know exactly where to buy them.

Today's families are smaller than in previous generations, and where there are two people earning salaries, there tends to be more disposable income. Some parents compensate for a lack of quality time spent with their kids by buying them things. This undermines messages about teaching kids the value of a dollar.

"Growing up, my family didn't have a lot of disposable income. My parents were able to provide for the necessities, but they could not afford the little extras like the cool brand of shoes or the hottest toy. I want my kids to have more than I had, and I want them to fit in. I feel guilty when I say no to something they want."

CELL PHONES — NEED OR WANT?

The way kids communicate with each other now — digitally rather than face to face — is radically different than it was when we were growing up. The average age at which kids get their first smartphones is around ten years old, but exposure to mobile devices begins much earlier.[10] We've all seen young kids on planes and in restaurants playing with iPads! Many parents are concerned that a phone will overtake their child's life, and their concern is well founded. Apps are designed to be addictive. For these reasons, every family has to decide for themselves at what age a cell phone is appropriate and affordable for their preteen.

At this stage, you're most likely to be the one paying the cell phone bill. However, your preteen should still be accountable for her data usage. Find the most appropriate package and be very clear about the cost of going over. If she does go over, she should be held accountable for paying the additional costs.

FAMILY DISCUSSION

Cell phones

- Is your kid responsible? Will they make sure the phone doesn't get lost, damaged, or stolen?
- Are they self-disciplined? Will they be able to follow rules about usage — for example, not using it in school and turning it off at night?
- Do they need it for safety reasons? Perhaps they walk to school alone or take public transit often. It may make both of you feel better to be reachable.

10. See www.todaysparent.com/family/parenting/an-age-by-age-guide-to-kids-and-smartphones/

MORE TEACHABLE MOMENTS

Grocery shopping provides lots of opportunities to teach responsible money management. While you're at home, let your kids help you make the shopping list. Let them see that you plan your meals in advance in order to avoid buying expensive takeout or restaurant meals. Remind them that feeding a family is a significant component of a household budget. Explain that shopping with a list means you're less likely to make impulse purchases and therefore keep within your budget. It also gives you ammunition when your kids start pestering you to buy all kinds of stuff: "It's not on our list!" Grocery shopping is also an opportunity to teach them to comparison shop, even if you're doing it online. Have them compare different brands, including store brands, to see which offer the best value. You can explain to them that the cheapest product doesn't always offer the best value if it isn't good quality. You may also want to point out that name brand products are more expensive than store brand products. This is because the name brand product includes the costs of marketing and advertising.

"I like to be thrifty. When my kids were young, they used to help me do the grocery shopping. First, we would go through the flyers and the coupons and see what was on sale. At the store, my kids would try to find items in our price range and look for the best value. I remember once asking my son to go get something we needed, but he came back empty-handed: 'Mom, it wasn't on sale.'"

DEBIT AND CREDIT CARDS

When your preteen opens a bank account, she'll get a bank card that can also be used as a debit card in stores.

As with ATM withdrawals, there are usually limits as to how much she can purchase by debit card per day. Make sure your child understands that she must have money in her account to cover debit purchases. Money must first be deposited before it can be spent.

Also, it never hurts to remind her not to disclose her PIN to anyone, although a PIN isn't always needed to authorize a purchase. Most debit (and credit) cards in Canada are embedded with chips that will allow your child to pay electronically, usually up to $100 for debit (and $250 for credit), just by tapping on a checkout reader. So remind her to be very careful not to lose her card!

Be sure your child understands the difference between a debit card and a credit card. If you haven't done so already, take the time to teach her what a credit card is and how it works (see Chapter 2, "At a Restaurant"). It's also a good idea to discuss the power of compounding, that the amount you owe keeps growing if you don't pay your balance off by the due date (see "Simple versus Compound Interest" in Chapter 4).

DIGITAL SPENDING: HOW DO YOU MAKE IT FEEL REAL?

Digital spending offers some unique challenges for parents. Just as spending your money doesn't feel real to your preteen, making digital purchases by tapping with their debit card or phone, or making in-app purchases, doesn't feel real either. Taking actual cash and handing it over to someone else definitely does! There is a psychological pain of loss associated with spending cash that we don't experience when we pay digitally.

Remind your child that even if they're not using cash, they're still spending real money, whether they're using their debit card, phone, a gift card, or your credit card or PayPal account. And if your kids do buy things online, consider having them reimburse you in cash.

Share

FOSTERING AN ATTITUDE OF GRATITUDE

In Chapter 1 we discussed how and why you're important role models for your kids. They don't absorb just your behaviour but your attitudes too. Fostering an attitude of gratitude begins with you showing appreciation for what you have instead of focusing on what you don't. (If you haven't already done so, take the **Role Model Self-Assessment** at the end of Chapter 1.) If you don't want your kids to have an attitude of entitlement and take things for granted, then you must continue to show them that you work hard for the money you make, you spend it carefully, you value the things you buy, and you look after them.

"I think you need to set up expectations for your kids early on. You can't give them everything.

They need to earn it. You need to start by being a good role model yourself. I was raised by a single mother, and growing up, my mother always kept us in the loop about our family finances. We knew that she could only afford to buy us our favourite toy once a year, and we respected that. We treated that toy very well."

HELPING THOSE LESS FORTUNATE

In normal times, it's not always easy to say no when your preteens ask for things and they often complain that they're "deprived." But it may be even harder to spend when money is tight. One way to put things into perspective for them, as we discussed in Chapter 1, is to show them the household budget, reminding them of all the other needs that have to be provided for. Another way is to help them realize that there are others less fortunate than they are, others they can help. While they may take for granted that they will always have clothes and shoes that fit, there are other children who are not so lucky.

"I get my kids to participate in deciding what to do with the toys and books they don't use anymore and the clothes that no longer fit. Together we go through their closets and take out any clothes that

they can't or don't wear anymore. Then we drop them off at a charity in our community. This teaches them that stuff — even their old stuff — has value, and people are grateful to receive it."

Invest

Although kids this age are too young to understand a lot about investing, here are two ways to introduce them to some basic concepts.

CASHFLOW, THE BOARD GAME — MONOPOLY ON STEROIDS!

We tend to focus on teaching kids how to work for money, rather than teaching kids how to make money work for them. After the Taylors had mastered Monopoly, they found a board game called Cashflow. You start in a typical nine-to-five job and embark on a journey to build up assets like property, stocks, businesses, and precious metals so you can get out of the rat race and start building wealth. By playing Cashflow as a family, the Taylors were able to learn valuable lessons and gain insights into personal finance and investing, including how they behave within investing scenarios, without having to put their actual money at risk. (There are versions of this game for adults and for kids.)

ENTREPRENEURSHIP REVISITED

Some service businesses, like babysitting or tutoring, don't require much from your preteen in the way of start-up capital. Everything they earn is pure profit. Others, like mowing lawns or snow shovelling, may require an upfront investment in equipment. Businesses that involve buying inventory and reselling it, like the proverbial lemonade stand, also require an upfront investment in materials.

KEY POINTS

- Between the ages of 9 and 12, your kids' understanding of the world is deeper than it was at younger ages. You can help them deepen their understanding of how money works too.
- The money habits that kids form in these years can be the foundation for how they relate to money when they're much older. Help them develop habits that are based on conscious decisions, not impulsive reactions.
- At this stage of their lives, kids are better able to grasp the rationale behind budgeting and to become increasingly accountable for how well they stick to their budget.
- As with younger kids, there are plenty of moments in everyday life that lend themselves to conversations about money when your kids are this age. But they're also old enough to benefit from more formal direction — for instance, going to the bank with you to set up their own savings account.

Teaching Teenagers

A Roadmap for Teens Thirteen to

Seventeen Years Old

The teenage years are a time of transition from carefree childhood to the adult world of responsibilities, including financial responsibilities. Ideally, you have been teaching your kids about money all along, beginning in elementary school and progressing as they entered middle school. But what if you haven't — is it too late? No, it's never too late to learn the basics of earn, save, spend, share, and invest. But this is a crucial time for your teen to develop sound money management skills. As parents, you must lead by example — like it or not, you are financial role models!

It can be difficult to communicate with your teenager about anything at this age, but when it comes to money, try not to make it a taboo subject in your home.

Your kid will learn best if you can manage to be open and adopt a positive attitude to discussing money. Be prepared to answer your teen's questions and speak to them as equals. Don't bore them with lectures — and always try to maintain your sense of humour!

FAMILY DISCUSSION

Money

You may want to initiate the conversation about money with some open-ended questions:

- What does money mean to you?
- What does it mean to have a lot of money?
- How much is a lot of money?
- What happens when you cannot pay back what you owe?

Earn

THEIR FIRST REAL JOB

Up until now, your kids have earned money by receiving an allowance, from birthday gifts, or as payment for doing odd jobs. Adolescence is usually the time when they get their first real job, earning money by working part-time during the year or full-time in the summer. Your teenagers may work in a grocery store or pharmacy, stocking shelves, or at a fast food restaurant. Unlike the odd jobs they worked in the past, these jobs will require them to have a Social Insurance Number (SIN), so that they can be paid, and a bank account (if they don't already have one). For the first time they will have a boss, co-workers, and shifts — in other words, a lot more responsibility.

You want your teen's first real job to be a positive experience for them. They will need your support as they make the transition from being dependent on you for money to making their own. Motivation is the key to a teenager's initiation to the working world. Encourage them to adopt a positive attitude toward work at a young age so they develop a strong work ethic. You are a role model in this area too, so be aware of your own attitude toward work. Do you wake up energized and excited to get to work, or do you experience a sense of dread at the thought of another workweek? Whether you realize it or not, they probably know how you really feel about your work.

It can be difficult for teenagers to find jobs because they usually don't have much work experience. They need to be determined and motivated when looking, and they'll need your support in their job search and your guidance in their choice of a job. Most jobs have minimum age requirements of 15 or 16 years. Some teens will be able to handle a part-time job during the school year and still get good grades; for others it may be too much — only you know what's right for your teen.

THINGS TO DO

Getting a job

Once your teen has decided to get a job, you can help by suggesting the following steps:

1. Apply for a Social Insurance Number and card.
   - Go to www.sdc.gc.ca and allow six weeks for the card to be processed.
2. Know what you're good at and what you want to do.
   - Look for jobs that will allow you to use your strengths and skills. You can discover your strengths by using an online strength assessment tool, many of which are free.
3. Start the job search.
   - Prepare a resume and cover letter (most teens get help with this in their careers class at school).
   - Use your network and online job boards to find opportunities, and don't be afraid to promote yourself.
4. Prepare for the interview.
   - Try to present yourself with confidence.
   - Dress appropriately.
5. Follow up.
   - Make sure your outgoing voice mail sounds professional.
   - Send out thank you emails.
   - Check in after a week if you haven't heard back.

HELPING THEM UNDERSTAND THEIR PAYCHEQUE

The first paycheque can be very exciting for your teen! It's worth taking a few minutes to go over the pay stub your teen receives with his cheque so he understands the difference between "gross" and "net" pay. Explain that employers are required by law to make certain deductions or "withholdings" directly from gross pay (the hourly wage or salary) and send these amounts straight to the government. These may include income tax, Employment Insurance (EI), and Canada Pension Plan (CPP) contributions. As a result, your kid's "net" or take-home pay may be quite a bit lower than they were expecting.

You may want to explain that in Canada we pay tax at graduated rates, meaning that the tax rate goes up as your income rises. Also, we pay income tax to both the federal and provincial governments. There is a tax credit called the Basic Personal Amount ($13,229 for the 2020 tax year and $13,808 for 2021, for most taxpayers). If your teen earns this amount or less in a year, their earnings are not subject to federal tax and generally no tax should be withheld at source.

They may be baffled by CPP and EI. Simply explain that they are programs run by the government, and every person who works must contribute to them. CPP pays benefits to seniors who qualify, and EI protects workers by paying out benefits to those who become unemployed. Make sure they know that their employer also contributes to EI and CPP on their behalf.

Sample Immigration Services, Inc., 55 Village Centre Pl. Mississauga ON, L5B 0E1				EARNINGS STATEMENT

Sample Name

EMPLOYEE ID	PERIOD ENDING	PAY DATE	CHECK NUMBER
212121	2021/08/23	2021/08/30	000012

INCOME	RATE	HOURS	CURRENT TOTAL	DEDUCTIONS	CURRENT TOTAL	YEAR TO DATE
REGULAR			2,000.00	CPP	92.34	1,569.78
				EI	32.36	550.12
				FED TAX	217.70	3,700.90
				INCOME TAX	111.94	1,902.98

CURRENT TOTAL	DEDUCTIONS
2,000.00	454.34

YTD GROSS	YTD DEDUCTIONS	YTD NET PAY	NET PAY
34,000.00	7,723.78	26,276.22	1,545.66

PAYING FOR GOOD GRADES

Some parents find it very difficult to motivate their kids to study. Out of frustration and desperation, they may be tempted to "bribe" their kids to get good grades. But this may give kids the wrong idea — that everything has a price and that they should be paid for every accomplishment. At this early stage, it's better to try to help teens find some intrinsic motivation, some drive within themselves to do their best. Focus on their strengths and the subjects they're good at. Success in these areas becomes self-reinforcing. You can also remind them that learning good study habits, like learning good money habits, will serve them well as they progress through school and hopefully on to higher learning.

"In our family, my parents rewarded us with 'bonuses' when we made the honour roll at school. But rather than give us the money, they put our bonuses into an RESP to encourage and motivate us to go to university."

ONLINE CONSIGNMENT SALES

Do people still hold garage sales? It seems like anyone with anything to sell these days does it online using eBay,

Craigslist, Kijiji, or social media sites. Looking around your house, you probably have lots of items that are perfectly good but are no longer useful to your family. Consider having your teen sell some of those items online. Remember the Three Cs we introduced in Chapter 1 — create, conserve, convert? Well, this is a great example of convert. Think of it as a consignment sale. They are selling items on your behalf and as a result are entitled to keep a portion of the proceeds of sale. Whether you split the proceeds fifty-fifty or some other way is entirely up to you and your teen — and it will be a good test of their negotiating skills! It's a win-win proposition — the more they are able to get for the item, the more you both make.

"My son is 16 and has been playing guitar since he was 9. We bought him his first electric guitar as a birthday gift, and for a long time it was suitable for his skill level. But as he progressed, he really wanted a better guitar. He did some research to figure out what he wanted to buy and what it would cost. Then we sat down to figure out how we were going to pay for it. My son came up with his own version of the Three Cs: he would create wealth by doing extra chores, he would conserve his allowance by spending less on snacks after school, and he would convert his old guitar into cash by selling it to a buyer he found online!"

Save

IS CASH STILL KING?

The expression "cash is king" is still conceptually valid in today's digital world, even if it's not literally true. It applies equally to businesses and to individuals. When you have cash or other financial resources, you are in command and you call the shots. You have the resources to ride out difficult times, and you also have the capital to take advantage of opportunities that arise. On the other hand, being in debt can weigh you down. The interest you carry on the debt combined with the debt itself is like an albatross around your neck. (As we discussed in Chapter 1, not all debt is bad. There is such a thing as good debt, i.e., debt incurred for the purpose of acquiring an asset that has the potential to go up in value, such as your house or other investments.)

The best place for your teen to save money is in the bank. Almost every teenager should have his or her own bank account. If your child expresses interest (pun intended), you can make sure they understand that the way a bank makes money is by earning a "spread." The interest rate they pay you on your savings is lower than the interest rate they charge on amounts that their customers borrow.

Help your teen to determine what type of account is best for them (chequing or savings). Investigate whether they still qualify for a youth account, as most fees are waived. At this stage, you can assume that your teen will be accessing the ATM on her own. Remind her that ATMs found in restaurants and most convenience stores charge very high fees. A $20 withdrawal may end up costing her $2.50 to $4 in fees. If she still uses cash regularly, encourage her to plan her cash needs ahead of time and use an ATM owned by her bank, where withdrawals are usually free. If, however, she's using debit more often, she should review the terms of her account to make sure she's not exceeding the number of free debit transactions per month and incurring additional fees.

Of course, teenagers can't apply for credit cards until they reach the age of majority, which is either 18 or 19, depending on their province of residence. However, they can benefit from learning about the responsible use of credit cards. We will revisit this topic in Chapter 5.

DIGITAL AND CRYPTOCURRENCIES

In Chapter 2, we introduced the concept of money as a medium of exchange, with banknotes and coins as examples of physical currency that younger kids could understand. Digital currency (also known as digital or electronic money) is another type of currency that has become much more prevalent, and which your teenagers are sure to encounter. Digital currencies are similar to physical currencies, but they can also allow for instantaneous, frictionless, and borderless transactions; they don't go through a central authority like the government or a central bank.

Cryptocurrencies are a type of digital currency, with Bitcoin being the best known and the largest. If your teens are interested in understanding Bitcoin, you can explain that it uses strong cryptography (hence the name) to secure financial transactions, controls the creation of additional units, and fluctuates in value. Transactions are recorded in a decentralized ledger (the blockchain) that is public and contains records of each and every transaction that takes place. Bitcoin isn't backed by the government.

USING PERSONAL VALUES TO SET SMART[11] GOALS

In Chapter 1, we introduced the idea of using your values to set meaningful goals. Values are the things in life that are most important to you, that you are willing to take a stand for. You can get a sense of what people value by the way they dress, how they spend their money, or how they interact with others. Values are intangible, but they are not invisible to others. You may think your kids will absorb your values about money by osmosis, be they power, friendship, connection, adventure, fun, or security. But as we suggested in Chapter 1, kids are exposed to a lot of conflicting messages about money, so it's important to be clear and explicit about your family values and how they impact your financial decisions. If they haven't done it already, get your kids

11. SMART goals are Specific, Measurable, Attainable and Action-oriented, Realistic, and Timely.

to try the **Values Validator** at the end of Chapter 1. Their values will help them prioritize their spending and set SMART savings goals.

FAMILY DISCUSSION

Goal setting

Discuss SMART goals with your kids. They are:

- Specific
- Measurable
- Attainable and Action-oriented
- Realistic
- Timely

When Emma Taylor completed the Values Validator, she determined that her top five values were adventure, friendship, health, academics, and security. She focused on adventure, doing new and interesting things, and developed a very meaningful SMART goal for herself. Here is Emma's goal-setting worksheet.

Top 5 Values	Top 5 Financial Goals	Make Specific, Measurable, Attainable, and Action-Oriented		48-Hour Plan What actions will you take in the next 48 hours?	Enlist Help Who will you share your goals with?	Time Frame When will you finish?
Adventure	Save up for a trip to Europe after high school graduation.	$3,000 will be needed by July 1, 2022.	Go online and research the cost of the trip. Calculate how much I can make if I work full-time over the next two summers and part-time during the school year.	Speak to my manager at work about adding shifts.	Discuss the travel budget with my parents and get their feedback.	In two years, I will need to book the airfare and have enough money saved for hotels, trains, food, and shopping.
Friendship						
Health						
Academics						
Security						

12. Adapted from The Purpose-Focused Financial Plan worksheet in *The Finish Rich Workbook*, David Bach (Toronto: Doubleday Canada, 2005).

For another example of a goal-setting worksheet, please see **Further Resources** at **robintaub.com**.

PAYING THEMSELVES FIRST — AND MAKING IT AUTOMATIC

Living within your means is arguably the most important lesson you can teach your kids. And the best way to teach it is to put your money where your mouth is: don't spend more than you make. Easier said than done, right? Wrong! You can make sure you don't spend more than you make by paying yourself first. And this is exactly what your teenager should be doing with the money he makes, too.

Every month, he should take a certain amount of money directly from his earnings and put it into savings. A rule of thumb is to save 10 percent of what you earn. If that seems like too much at first, then begin with 5 percent. If 10 percent is easily achieved, then increase it to 15 or 20 percent. To make sure it happens, have him set it up as an automatic transfer. Save him from himself — he will able to spend only what remains. Having a SMART goal that he's saving for, one that ties back to his values, will make saving meaningful and rewarding and will increase his chances of success.

Spend

Once your kids hit their teen years, they tend to want to spend all their time with their friends. Many teenagers enjoy going shopping and hanging out at the mall or downtown, even with social distancing in place. (However, some may choose to do their shopping online and their socializing in small groups or bubbles). They will still probably go out of their way to avoid you! You don't have as many teachable moments as you did when they were younger, when they would accompany you on shopping excursions. They are much more interested in the opinions of their friends (in real life and on social media) when it comes to consuming, but they are also better able to assert their individuality than they were just a few years earlier. However, as long as they are still living under your roof, you can find the right time to instill good spending habits.

ALLOWANCE: INCREASED FINANCIAL RESPONSIBILITY

Whether your teen is working or not, they may still need an allowance. But use it to begin gradually transferring more financial responsibilities to them. They can use the allowance to cover their basic needs and some of their wants. As we will discuss under **Budgeting**, the budget should be the basis for determining their allowance, which should be given to your teen regularly — weekly, biweekly, or monthly.

As with your younger children, you may choose to use an app to pay your child's allowance. Anything that's easy for you to set up and use, and that is also engaging and informative for your teens, is worth trying.

If your teen is also working, should they be allowed to spend the money they earn however they want? Teens want to be independent, and you should let them make their own money choices and live with the consequences. But first give them some guidance and support or they are liable to make some unwise decisions.

BUDGETING

Teens may not have much overhead if they live at home because you're still taking care of most of their needs. As a result, they may not know what their lives really cost. A mistake that teenagers often make, especially if they don't have savings goals, is to use all their income on discretionary spending.

There is no shortage of items tempting your teen to spend their money: video games, electronics, clothes, shoes, junk food, concerts, etc. These temptations can be difficult to resist at any age. While kids can technically get away with blowing their money at this age, it establishes a bad habit that may be hard to break once they get older and they do have to worry about rent, food, transportation, and utilities — all the mundane essentials.

As we mentioned in Chapter 3, it's a good idea to regularly review the budget with your teen to see if it needs fine-tuning. The review process also ensures that she feels accountable for staying within budget, and it can provide an explanation as to why she was under or over budget. Just like in the "real world," things will come up from time to time, and your teen may decide she wants to rob Peter to pay Paul. In other words, she wants to redirect funds from one budget category to another. That's fine — all budgets are flexible — as long as she does it intentionally and can account for it. See the **Teen Budget Template** at the end of this chapter.

THINGS TO DO

Budget

- Work with your teen to create a budget. (If your kid has been budgeting from a younger age, all the better!)
- Calculate a reasonable amount for their cell phone, transportation, and clothing, being careful to hold your ground on needs versus wants.
- Work out an entertainment budget. Although they may be spending less of their entertainment budget outside of the home, they may still be spending money on streaming services for music and TV, on-demand movies and video games.
- Have your kid save receipts so she can keep track of what she spends and you can review the details.

Especially with teens, it's important to let them make mistakes and learn their lessons. Although the stakes are higher than they were at a younger age, we're still not talking about thousand-dollar mistakes. Letting them waste their money on something they don't need, or that's of low quality, can teach them a lot about value, but only if you take the time to discuss it.

"My 16-year-old daughter went through a 'Starbucks phase' where she was stopping often on her way home from school and buying fancy, expensive coffees. She didn't realize how these little purchases were adding up. When the weekend rolled around, she made plans with her friends to see a movie. But as she got ready to go, she checked her wallet and realized she had spent most of her money and didn't have enough to see a movie. She wanted me to give her the shortfall, but I wouldn't. I wanted her to learn that when you make choices about how to spend your money, you have to live with the consequences — even if it meant 'ruining' her social life."

TRACKING SPENDING

In Chapter 1, we explained why it's so important for you to track spending: it's the only way to find out where your money is really going, and it makes you more aware of your spending habits. It's a great reality check for your kid, too. They often think they're spending according to the plan — until they face the numbers and see that their tracking shows a very different spending pattern! And as with all of us, being more mindful of their spending can motivate them to make better spending choices going forward.

The Taylors used the jar system to teach Emma to track her spending. She no longer had a piggy bank, of course, but she had three jars in her room labelled "clothing," "entertainment," and "transportation." Emma would allocate her budget to each of the three categories. As she spent money from the jar, she would replace the money spent with a receipt. She could see quite easily how much money was left in her budget in each category at any time. When she got to the end of the money in a jar, she could no longer spend in that category, unless she chose to take it from a different category.

But there's a whole world of ways for your kids to spend money without using cash. Digital payment systems, like PayPal and Interac e-Transfer, let them send, request, and receive money, and Apple Pay allows them to make purchases in stores, in apps, and on the web. As discussed in Chapter 3, when your kids pay for things by card or phone, rather than using cold, hard cash, they feel less of a sting and assign less value to a purchase.

DIGITAL TOOLS

Although the Taylors used a very low-tech system with Emma, because she was mostly spending cash, as we move toward a more cashless world, the tools we use need to keep pace. There are lots of different apps that can help your teen manage their finances, including the mobile banking app from your teen's bank. In addition to letting them view account balances, pay bills, or transfer money, the app also contains tools to track spending by category and create budgets. You can also set up real-time spending notifications that let you know if you're spending more or less than usual. So even if your teen is not using cash, getting a spending notification will make it more vivid and will help them feel like they're spending real money. Apps may appeal to teens who are already using their phones to do just about everything else.

In addition to monitoring spending, many apps contain tools that allow your teen to set goals and monitor their progress toward achieving them. Using mobile banking to manage their money and monitor their finances is a good habit for your teen to get into early.

NEEDS VERSUS WANTS AGAIN

During the teenage years, your kid may start to develop a sense of entitlement, demanding the very latest shoes, clothes, cell phones, and laptops. Just like younger kids, teens need to be reminded of the difference between needs and wants. Remind them to ask themselves that all-important question: Do I need it, or would it just be nice to have? Help them understand that they have to take their resources (time and money) into account when making purchasing decisions.

Raising money-smart kids in a world that stresses instant gratification and consumption can be challenging. Social media and "FOMO" (the fear of missing out) are the new peer pressure, and even kids feel like they have to spend to keep up appearances online of "living their best life."

It can be shocking to see how sophisticated some teens' tastes are and to watch them covet certain brands. This can be an opportunity to talk to them about marketing and branding. Show them that companies spend a lot of money marketing their products to convince you that you "need" them. Teens are subject to as much, if not more, media and advertising as younger kids. As parents, you can help your teen think critically and skeptically about the messages they get.

Studies are showing that spending too much time on Instagram and other social media and making upward social comparisons can really hurt your kids. Comparing, coveting, and competing with their peers can lead to feelings of envy, bad moods, and dissatisfaction with life. It increases stress levels. It can also lower self-control, which may lead to overspending.

For these and other reasons, you may want to implement some restrictions around cell phone use. In some households, phones are turned off at 9:00 p.m., not stored overnight in bedrooms, and forbidden during family meals. There are also screen-free periods on the weekend so kids can focus on other activities. Once again, you should lead by example and try to follow similar rules.

"I get really excited if I'm about to buy something new, but after I buy it, it never makes me as happy as I think it's going to."

A SUSTAINABLE APPROACH TO FINANCIAL RESPONSIBILITY

Compared to younger kids, teenagers seem to be more aware of, and more concerned about, the impact their consumption has on the environment. You can use this concern to guide them. For example, remind them that constantly demanding new and improved things takes its toll on the environment; excessive, unnecessary driving causes pollution; and being careless by leaving lights on wastes electricity. You don't want to become a nag, but helping them develop a mindset of sustainability may moderate their consumption habits and lead them to make more responsible choices that are respectful of the environment.

SPENDING WISELY

Even though teens (hopefully!) have more maturity and self-discipline than younger kids, their brains are still developing, and they still often tend to act on impulse — but you can help. Encourage your teen to shop around and compare prices as a way to stretch their budget and get more for their hard-earned money. Help them look for coupon codes, sales, or promotions. Let them see how much they can save by taking a patient and disciplined approach to shopping.

"Money was tight in my family when I was growing up. At Christmastime, my mom used to give my siblings and me each $10. She told us to use the $10 to buy a Christmas gift for each member of the family. Ten dollars isn't a lot of money, so you really had to shop wisely to stretch your budget. This was a very good skill to learn."

STORED VALUE CARDS

Because they can be difficult to shop for, teens tend to get stored value cards, like gift cards, as presents. Teach them to read the fine print: some gift cards have expiry dates. Also, the cards tend to get forgotten in the back of their wallets unless kids are proactive about using them. Get them to make a list of all the gift cards they have and their remaining balances and to make a plan to spend them before they expire. And remind them that the cards are usually not replaceable, so they should be sure to keep them in a place where they will not lose them.

"When my kids, ages 8 and 13, get gift cards for their birthdays, I buy the gift cards off them and give them cash instead. And I make them save half. If they had their way, they would use their gifts cards immediately to buy toys or video games that they don't really need. But then it feels like free money, not real money, and my kids don't respect it as much. Easy come, easy go."

NEGOTIATING AND BARGAINING

In some places in the world, negotiating and bargaining when making purchases is the norm — in fact, it's expected. Not so in Canada. In most retail stores, especially large chains, the price as displayed is the price you pay at the cash, unless it's on sale. However, at some markets, you may be able to get a discount if you ask. It always pays to ask whether the price displayed is actually the best price available.

And don't forget to tell your teen to budget for sales tax when buying something. Some may not realize that taxes are not normally included in the price of goods but are additional costs. In some provinces, the total sales tax can be as high as 15 percent.

TIPPING

Next time you are out for dinner with your teen, talk to them about tipping. They may already know about it, but if they don't, it's pretty certain they'll need to know before too long — they'll soon be going out to eat on their own with friends. They may not know that servers rely on tips because their hourly wage is very low. You can teach them that the tip is calculated on the total before tax and is usually 15–20 percent for good to excellent service.

Many restaurants, and even takeout food and coffee shops, have tipping built into their point of sales terminals. Often, the suggested tip will start at 18 percent and will be calculated automatically on top of the sales tax. Remind your teen that they can always choose to tip a lower amount or to not tip at all, especially on takeout.

Share

RAISING MONEY AT SCHOOL

Wander the halls of your teenager's school and you will see flyers announcing Terry Fox runs and United Way bake sales — you name it! Schools encourage their student bodies to get involved in fundraising and donating money to causes that they're passionate about. The school wants to foster a sense of community and the satisfaction involved when you give back, and many students spend time volunteering for community service projects as well.

If your teen connects with one of the fundraising projects going on at school, encourage him to get involved. But if nothing resonates with him, perhaps he could establish a new fundraising initiative at the school by speaking to a teacher or the vice-principal.

"One of the most successful and popular fundraising events at my school was Faculty Follies. We approached three well-known and well-liked teachers at our school, and we asked them to participate. Their role was to commit to do something outrageous, like grow a moustache and dye it pink, dress up as a Star Wars character, or shave their head. Then we set up three large jars and asked students to contribute spare change toward the outrageous act that they most wanted to see.

There were no costs involved, so we were able to donate 100 percent of the proceeds to charity. The 'winning' teacher had to dress up like Darth Vader and teach all of his classes in a Star Wars costume!"

RAISING MONEY FOR SCHOOL

Sometimes, the beneficiary of the school's fundraising efforts is the school itself. Schools have budgets too, and there never seems to be enough money to go around. Our public schools are funded by the government, but the cutbacks in recent years have left schools scrambling to make ends meet. Rather than make further cuts to programs, schools often establish foundations and have fundraising campaigns.

"Last fall, my son's high school had an unusual fundraiser. Rather than the typical fun fair, they held an event called 24-Hour Survival. Each student had to raise at least $25 for the chance to spend 24 hours camping out on the back field of the school! The field was divided into 'girls' camp' and 'boys' camp.' They brought portable camping stoves so they could cook their meals, and they

slept in tents. (Our son begged us to deliver a pizza to his tent!) The event was sanctioned by the school and supervised by school staff. It was definitely one of the highlights of his school year!"

Invest

INVESTING FOR SHORT- AND MEDIUM-TERM GOALS

Most teenagers don't have a lot of money to invest. Whatever money they're not spending on immediate purchases, they're probably just stashing in a savings account to spend at a later date. But as they start to develop longer-term goals, they need to understand the relationship between goals and investments, as well as some investing basics. Help them understand that their goals or investment objectives, the length of time they have to reach their goals (investment time horizon), and their appetite for taking risks (risk tolerance) will determine what type of investment is appropriate in the circumstances. We will cover this in more detail in Chapter 5.

A short-term goal means you will need the money in a few weeks or a few months (say to buy a gift) and a bank account is generally the most appropriate savings vehicle. You will earn a low rate of interest, but the funds are 100 percent safe and liquid, meaning easily cashable. Short of the bank collapsing, you will always be able to get your money when you need it.

With a medium-term goal, say one to five years, you have more investment options. You can purchase a term deposit or Guaranteed Investment Certificate (GIC) at the bank with a term that matches your goal. The longer the term, the longer the money is locked in and the more interest you will earn; also, the interest rates on term deposits and GICs are higher than the interest rates on savings accounts. The interest earned will encourage your child to save, as it helps them reach their goal faster. The fact that a GIC cannot normally be cashed in before it matures reinforces the concept of delayed gratification.

Say your fifteen-year-old son has saved a substantial amount over the years (from birthday money, holiday gifts, babysitting, odd jobs, etc.) and is saving for his first year in residence at university in three years. He could purchase a three-year term deposit or GIC with a fixed rate of interest, compounded annually. He will know exactly what he will earn, assuming he holds the GIC until maturity. Again, the principal is guaranteed, so there is no way he can lose his investment. But the funds are frozen for this three-year period, and penalties apply if the investment is cashed before the maturity date.

A longer-term goal requires different planning. You can choose investments with growth potential. Because you have a much longer time horizon, you can take advantage of time and let compounding work for you. With these criteria, you have many more investment options available, which we will cover in Chapter 5.

"I taught my teenager about the 'Rule of 72.' It's a simple formula that tells you how long it will take to double your money with compound interest. Divide the number 72 by the interest rate you earn each year. For example, if you have $1,000 invested at 6 percent compounded annually, divide 72 by 6 to get 12. You will double your money in 12 years."

SIMPLE VERSUS COMPOUND INTEREST

Simple interest is when the bank pays you a stated rate of interest for a stated period of time on your original deposit, which is called the principal. Let's say the bank is offering a savings account at 3 percent simple interest, and you deposit $100. Once a year, the bank will pay you 3 percent of $100, or $3, and add it to the balance in your savings account. After one year, your balance would be $103. At the end of the second year, you would earn an additional $3 of interest and your balance would be $106. After ten years, you would have earned $30 of interest and have a balance of $130. After 20 years, you would have $160.

Compound interest is when you earn interest on your

interest. The magic of compound interest is that it allows your savings to grow much more quickly. Let's say the bank is offering a savings account at 3 percent interest compounded annually. This means that the interest you earn each year is added to your principal and becomes the new basis for calculating the following year's interest. As in the example above, you receive $3 in the first year, so at the end of the year you have $103. But here's the difference: at the end of the second year, interest is calculated at 3% of $103, so you now earn $3.09, giving you a balance of $106.09. After ten years, you would have earned $34.39 and would have a balance of $134.39 versus $130 with simple interest. After 20 years, you would have $180.61 — that's $20.61 more than you would have earned with simple interest.

Simple Interest vs. Compound Interest

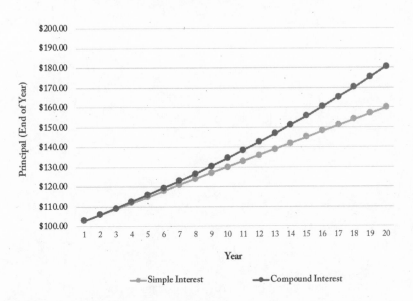

When you are earning a higher interest rate and have a longer period of time to invest, compounding can make a huge difference. That's why it's so important for kids to develop good saving habits early — to take full advantage of the power of compounding and let their money work for them, rather than the other way around.

This is also a good time to explain that compound interest is a double-edged sword. It's great when you're a saver and it's working for you. But if you're a borrower, it works just as hard against you. Interest on debt compounds quickly and becomes quite burdensome, especially when interest rates are very high, as they are on credit card balances.

KEY POINTS

- Your kid's first real job presents a great opportunity to introduce them to the working world — going over their first pay stub with them and explaining about income tax, CPP, and EI teaches a lot about how our society works.
- Teens are not too young to set meaningful financial goals; the clearer their goals, the more likely they are to achieve them.
- School-sponsored programs can be a good opportunity for kids to learn about giving back. Sometimes they can even initiate a charitable program and get the school to endorse it.
- Some teens may be interested in learning some of the basic concepts of investing; the sooner they learn them, the better prepared they'll be when they actually have money to invest.

RESOURCES

Teen Budget Template

Monthly Budget for Teens			
Category	Monthly Budget	Actual Amount	Difference
INCOME	Estimate Your Income	Your Actual Income	
Wages/Income Paycheque, allowance, birthday money, etc.			
Interest Income From savings account			
INCOME SUBTOTAL			
EXPENSES	Estimate Your Expenses	Your Actual Expenses	
Savings Savings account			
Bills Taxes — from paycheque			
Food/snacks			
Transportation			
Clothing and other shopping			

Cell phone			
Entertainment (e.g., movies, restaurants, video games, music)			
EXPENSES SUBTOTAL			
NET INCOME			

Goal-Setting Worksheet[13]

Top 5 Values	Top 5 Financial Goals	Make Specific, Measurable, Attainable, and Action-Oriented	48-Hour Plan What actions will you take in the next 48 hours?	Enlist Help Who will you share your goals with?	Time Frame When will you finish?
Example: Security	Increase net worth by 10 percent next year	Increase contributions to RRSP by $200 per paycheque	Call benefits person at work; change contributions plan by Friday	Call Pete (financial advisor) to review investment options in RRSP	In two weeks, the new investment plan will begin
Family					
Health					
Self-realization / self-development					
Community					

13. Adapted from the Purpose-Focused Financial Plan worksheet in *The Finish Rich Workbook*, David Bach (Toronto: Doubleday Canada, 2005).

Teaching Emerging Adults

A Roadmap for Young Adults Eighteen

to Twenty-One Years Old

Your son or your daughter will always be your child, but at this stage, they hardly seem like children any longer! They have finished high school and have emerged from adolescence into young adulthood. They have now reached the age of majority, which means they can legally take on more responsibilities: voting, entering into contracts, serving on a jury, or even marrying! They may also have more financial responsibilities, such as filing a tax return, opening an investment account or paying for college or university.

Post-secondary study is a good example of the concept of "opportunity cost" — the most valuable alternative you give up by choosing another, mutually exclusive option. Some kids at this age may be tempted to start working full-time and earning money rather than going on to do further studying. But while students who go on to university or college give up the opportunity to earn income right away, they expect that they will more than make up for it with higher earning potential after they graduate. Arguably, a university education more than pays for itself over time, and the opportunity costs in this case are minimal. In other situations, the opportunity costs may be significant. Say your child is considering two very different career paths: investment banker or social worker. The opportunity cost of choosing a career as a social worker rather than an investment banker is quite high in terms of forgone earnings. It may still be the right choice for your son or daughter, based on many other considerations, but encourage them to think carefully about alternatives and to consider the opportunity costs when making decisions.

"The more you learn, the more you earn."

— Warren Buffet

"My parents made me and my brothers get summer jobs working in a factory or doing manual labour. They wanted us to appreciate the value of an education and the opportunities it afforded us. After just a few days on a construction site, it was very clear to me that I wanted a stimulating career, one that was more mental than physical."

Earn

Your kid may be one of the fortunate ones; that is, they may know they can count on you to pay for their university education, which allows them the luxury of not working and gives them more time to focus on their studies during the school year. Or maybe your kid will be working part-time during the school year or full-time during the summer to help pay for university. If your kid didn't work as a teenager, you may want to go back to Chapter 4 and read the sections entitled "Their First Real Job" and "Helping Them Understand Their Paycheque." This is also a good time to talk to them about the responsibility of filing a tax return.

Throughout high school, Emma Taylor worked part-time at the Gap with her friend Allison. After graduation, Emma went to university out of town. Allison's family couldn't afford to send her away to school, so she lived at home and went to university. She also needed to keep working to help pay her tuition. Allison debated the pros and cons of keeping her job at the Gap. On the one hand, she had a track record of good performance and she had a little seniority, plus she wouldn't have to embark on a job search. On the other hand, as Emma pointed out, she might be limiting herself if she stayed. Prospective employers want people who have had experience at a variety of jobs in different fields. Allison agreed that different work experience would be good — she knew she didn't want to work at her Gap job forever — so she decided to look for a more challenging, better-paying job in her area of interest, using the tips outlined in Chapter 4. She ended up finding a position at the university, which employs a lot of students in different administrative, service, and teaching-related positions.

WHY FILE A TAX RETURN?

Some kids may not see the point of filing a tax return, especially if they haven't made very much money. If you are a resident of Canada for all or part of a tax year, you must file a tax return if you either owe tax or you think you may be entitled to a refund. Generally, you must file your return and pay your taxes by April 30 of the year following the tax year. As we discussed in Chapter 4, if your kid's taxable income falls under the Basic Personal

Amount then it's unlikely that they will owe tax.

We will discuss RRSPs and TFSAs in the next section.

TAX BREAKS FOR STUDENTS

Students are entitled to a tax credit for their tuition fees, which can be used to reduce any income taxes they owe.

There are rules that set out eligible expenses, and form T2202A, Tuition and Enrolment Certificate, must be completed. You can learn more by visiting the Canada Revenue Agency's website at www.canada.ca/en/revenue-agency/services/forms-publications/publications/p105.html.

Your child must claim the tuition first, even if you are the one paying. But if your child doesn't need all of the credit to reduce his or her income (e.g., because it's already below the Basic Personal Amount), then up to $5,000 can be transferred to your return to reduce your taxes (or to a grandparent). The credit can also be carried forward indefinitely and claimed in any future year.

If your child is moving to attend full-time post-secondary studies, they may be able to claim eligible moving expenses if:

- they receive scholarships and bursaries while at school that are included in their income; and
- they are moving at least 40 kilometres closer to attend school.

SCHOLARSHIPS AND BURSARIES

If your child receives a scholarship, fellowship, or bursary, the income will not be subject to tax if she is enrolled in an educational program as a full-time qualifying student. If your child is a part-time qualifying student, the scholarship exemption is equal to the tuition paid plus the costs of program-related materials. Details on the calculation can be found at www.canada.ca/en/revenue-agency/services/forms-publications/publications/p105/p105-students-income-tax-2016.html#chart.

Save

Some young adults decide to work full-time after high school, which means they are in a position to begin a savings program or to contribute more to a savings program that they'd started earlier. On the other hand, if your child is attending university or college, these are likely to be spending, not saving, years. She may have some short-term savings goals from time to time, but if she's earning any money, most of it is probably being spent on university tuition, books, and living costs. Your kid probably has a savings and/or a chequing account for managing day-to-day spending; if you haven't done so already, review the basic mechanics of managing a bank account, which we covered in Chapters 3 and 4. It's also worth the time to investigate whether your bank offers a special account for post-secondary students. If they do, your child may be entitled to services at discounted prices. Because you have already introduced your kid to the topic of income tax, take this opportunity to discuss using tax-advantaged savings vehicles as a way to minimize taxes.

TAX-ADVANTAGED SAVINGS

TAX-FREE SAVINGS ACCOUNT

A TFSA is a special savings vehicle for Canadians aged 18 or older. The annual contribution limit is currently $6,000 (indexed for inflation in $500 increments). Contributions to the account are *not* tax-deductible — they come out of after-tax earnings. However, income earned inside the account isn't subject to tax, nor are amounts withdrawn. If you withdraw an amount from your account, you can re-contribute that amount in the following year, in addition to that year's limit. If you don't have the funds to contribute, you can carry forward that amount indefinitely.

For these reasons, a TFSA is a very flexible tool for saving. It can be used to save for a down payment on a house or for an emergency fund, for example. Once you decide what you are saving for, you can choose the appropriate investments to hold, and any income is earned tax-free, allowing your savings to grow more quickly. We will discuss investing later in this chapter.

REGISTERED RETIREMENT SAVINGS PLAN

If your kid's income doesn't all have to go toward college or university expenses, starting an RRSP can be a good idea. Make sure they know the basics of how RRSPs work. An RRSP is a savings vehicle created by the government to help Canadians save for retirement. Unlike a

TFSA, amounts contributed to an RRSP *are* tax-deductible — they come out of pre-tax income, not after-tax earnings. The funds inside an RRSP are invested, and the investment income earned inside an RRSP isn't subject to tax. This means the investments can grow more quickly to help you reach your long-term goals. And remember, the power of compounding means that even a little bit saved early and often can make a big difference over time.

You must have earned income in order to contribute to an RRSP. There are rules about how much you can contribute each year, and you must file a tax return. The funds are not taxed until withdrawn at retirement, unless you decide to take the funds out early. There is a special exception for withdrawals made by a first-time home-buyer to purchase or build a qualifying home. In that scenario, you may withdraw up to $35,000 tax-free from your RRSP, but you must repay the money to your RRSP within 15 years.

THE "LATTE FACTOR"[14]

Saving money is challenging for most people, especially for students, who may feel like they're living a bare-bones existence in order to make ends meet. If your kids (or you) are looking to save a few dollars every week, you may want to examine your "latte factor." Everybody has one — it's those little indulgences and the wasteful

---

14. davidbach.com/

spending that you could either cut back on or eliminate altogether. Examples are fancy coffees, monthly subscriptions for apps or delivery services, or fast food. Giving up unhealthy and expensive habits like smoking is another great example. We often don't even realize how much we're actually spending on these little purchases, but they add up! Changing your habits may mean more money to pay for tuition and other costs of living.

Spend

When your child decides to go to university or another post-secondary institution, they're taking the first big step toward independence, a career, and financial security. It can be quite a challenging time, especially if they'll be living away from home in a different town or city for the first time. And because the cost of a university education is substantial, financial planning will be required.

PAYING FOR POST-SECONDARY EDUCATION

There are different ways to finance a university education, and they're not mutually exclusive. Depending on your circumstances, you may find yourself using some combination of your savings, which may take the form of withdrawals from an RESP; your current earnings/cash flow; scholarships or grants your child may receive; your child's savings; or their own earnings.

Finally, there are loans — either student loans or amounts borrowed from a personal line of credit or from other sources. This kind of debt is an example of good debt; a university education is an investment in your child's future career and earning power. However, they still need a plan to pay off that debt within a reasonable period of time. Carrying that much debt may delay or alter other goals, such as travelling, buying a house, or getting married.

If your child does get student loans, under the *Canada Student Loans Act*, the *Canada Students Financial Assistance Act*, or similar provincial or territorial government laws, they can claim most of the interest paid as a tax credit. If they don't use the credit, they can carry it forward for five years. The tax credit cannot be transferred to anyone else, even if someone else paid the interest on the loan. Also, they cannot claim interest paid on any other kind of loan, such as a personal loan or line of credit.

Perhaps an ideal solution to the issue of paying for university is a co-op program, which also gives participants valuable work experience. Many universities offer these programs (even during COVID-19) and help arrange the placements, which are usually for one semester. Students are paid for their work during that period and return to school at the end of the placement. Although working in a co-op program may mean it will take longer for the student to graduate (since students don't normally get credits for their work terms), the additional income is necessary for many kids to complete their education. And the practical experience can be invaluable: these placements often lead to permanent job offers if the student performs well, as well as providing opportunities to expand their professional networks. Even in the absence of a job offer, co-op placements give the student an opportunity for some real-world experience in his chosen field and can help him make a more informed career choice.

IS YOUR KID PREPARED TO BE ON HER OWN?

In Chapter 4 we introduced budgeting for teens, getting them used to the responsibility of managing their money, even though you were still taking care of most of their needs. Once they emerge into adulthood, whether into the workforce or off to university, they will need to be even more in control of their financial situation. They will need to know what is coming in and what is going out as they try to balance the inflow and outflow.

Your child should get into the habit of tracking his spending — it's really the only way to bring awareness to where the money is going. The accountability that comes with careful tracking can lead to making better spending choices. It will also let him compare his actual spending to his budget, to see where he's on track or where he may be over or under budget. Budgets are dynamic, and they need to be reviewed regularly — and sometimes revised.

What do you do if your kid keeps running out of money every month? First, review the budget and the actual spending to try to identify the problem area. If there is enough money to cover the basics (the fixed expenses), the problem may be discretionary spending on things like ordering in, taking out food and entertainment. Remember the three Cs — **create, convert,** and **conserve** — which we discussed in Chapter 1. He may have to cut back on some of these expenses or make more money.

"I got through university by taking full advantage of student discounts and always asking if there was a student rate for things like haircuts, gym memberships, or theatre tickets. I also got into the habit of using coupons or two-for-one promotions when I went out for dinner with my friends. And whenever we felt like seeing a movie, we made sure to go to the 'cheap Tuesday' shows!"

Budget

- Encourage your child to create a realistic budget — based on weekly, biweekly, or monthly amounts — using the **Post-Secondary Student Budget** at the end of this chapter.
- Remind them that it's better to be conservative in their planning than to run out of money:
    - Caution them not to overstate income.
    - Remind them to be specific and realistic about expense categories.
    - Be sure to include unusual expenses that may occur only once a year (such as moving costs, insurance, or holiday gifts).

CREDIT CARDS REVISITED

Once your child has reached the age of majority in your province, she can get her own credit card. A credit card can be very helpful in case of emergency. (No, joining her friends for dinner or shopping online isn't an emergency!) If your kid has been using *your* credit card for the last few years and isn't the one paying the bills, they may be quite naive about the responsible use of credit cards. If they get their own card, make sure the credit limit is low and try to find a card with no fees. Some cards even provide student discounts on purchases.

Credit is very easy to get and use. Many financial institutions offer credit cards specifically targeted to students, and they're marketed heavily on campuses. Paying by credit card is so convenient that it practically encourages spending. If you had to go to a bank and line up at the teller to take out cash every time you wanted to buy something, you would probably spend a lot less. These days, it's easy to withdraw cash from all the conveniently located ATMs, but it's even easier to just whip out a credit card or phone, then tap and worry about it later.

Once again, the best way to teach your kids to use credit cards responsibly is to model this behaviour yourself. Let them know that you pay off your credit card balance each month. Explain to them that the credit card is used for convenience, but that it's a very expensive way to buy things you can't afford.

"I was really happy about the new regulations requiring credit card companies to provide information on the time it would take to fully repay the balance if only the minimum payment is made every month. I read my kids the paragraph at the top of my most recent monthly statement for my credit card, which charges 20 percent interest: 'The estimated time to pay your $1,526.57 balance in full if you pay only the Minimum Payment each month is: 12 years and

2 months.' That's a rude awakening — my kids were in a state of shock — I think the message really hit home!"

---

flyer miles or cash-back payments.
- They can be used to pay for online purchases.

Discuss the risks and disadvantages of credit cards:

- They can damage your credit rating if you miss payments or your payments are late.
- They're more expensive than personal lines of credit because the interest rate charged is much higher.
- If not used responsibly, credit cards can lead to increased spending and bad debt.

If you feel your child is ready for the responsibility of a credit card, encourage him to take the time to choose the right credit card. The Financial Consumer Agency of Canada has excellent resources about credit cards and other financial topics at www.canada.ca/en/services/finance/debt.html.

FRAUD, SCAMS, AND IDENTITY THEFT

Fraud can take many forms, including scams involving fake emails or websites, identity theft, credit card fraud, and debit card fraud. Anyone can be a victim of fraud, and it's often costly — in terms of financial losses and in the time it takes to clear your record. Teach your young adult how to protect herself and her financial information with the following tips.

PREVENTING IDENTITY THEFT

Identity theft occurs when your personal information or identity is stolen for the purpose of accessing your financial accounts to steal your assets or incur debt in your name. Take precautions to protect your personal information at home, in public, on the phone, and online.

THINGS TO DO/WHAT NOT TO DO

Identity theft

- Never provide personal information to anyone unless you know and trust the person and understand why they need it.
- Never email or text your personal information.
- Keep documents such as birth certificates, passports, or Social Insurance Number cards in a secure and safe place — not in your wallet.
- Use only secure websites.
- Update your antivirus software regularly.
- Shred all documents that include your personal financial information, e.g., old bank statements and credit card statements.

PREVENTING CREDIT OR DEBIT CARD FRAUD

Credit and debit card fraud occurs when your credit/

debit card information or your PIN is stolen and used to make unauthorized purchases or transactions. This is yet another reason to set up notifications for real-time spending in your mobile banking app.

THINGS TO DO/WHAT NOT TO DO

Credit and debit card fraud

- Get a credit/debit card with chip technology. The embedded microchip is encrypted and virtually impossible to replicate.
- Don't share your credit/debit card or PIN.
- Never leave your credit/debit card unattended (or in your car's glove compartment), and make sure you get it back after payment.
- Cover the keypad when entering your PIN.
- Check your statements every month (or more frequently online) for errors or unauthorized transactions. Notify your bank or other financial institution immediately if something is amiss.
- Destroy cards you no longer need or use.

A NOTE ABOUT SOCIAL MEDIA

The popularity of social media sites makes it very easy for fraudsters to obtain personal information that can be used to decode passwords. Also, announcing your upcoming vacation or attendance at an event on a specific evening is like drawing a map to an empty apartment or house. You may come home to find your valuables missing, including the priceless personal information someone needs to steal your identity.

Share

VOLUNTEERING YOUR TIME

Most students don't have much money for themselves, let alone enough to give away to others. But sharing isn't always about money — sometimes it's about volunteering your time and talents to help others. The idea of community service isn't new — most students are now required to do some volunteering in order to graduate from high school. Although it's not usually mandatory in post-secondary studies, many students, despite the time pressures from their studies, choose to volunteer for two reasons — because volunteering aligns with their values, and because of the many benefits they receive. Depending on the type of volunteer work they do, students can expand their network, learn new skills, gain work-related experience, have an adventure, and feel good about giving back.

When looking for volunteer work, one of the most important considerations is passion. If your child doesn't already know what he or she is passionate about, ask them to complete or review their **Values Validator** (at the end of Chapter 1). This exercise will help them clarify what's really important to them, which will lead them to causes or organizations that they really care about. When you are not being paid for your time and efforts, passion is essential in order to remain committed. Before your child commits to a specific organization, it's a good idea for them to make sure they know exactly what the organization expects from them in terms of the nature and quantity of work involved. Depending on how formal the organization is, they may even want to get it in writing, so there are no misunderstandings later on.

PHILANTHROPY IS A FAMILY AFFAIR

In families where philanthropy is a key family value, the importance of sharing is taught at an early age and carried through to young adulthood.

"When my kids were young, they each had a charity piggy bank, and part of their allowance always went in there. When they became older, I set up a donor-advised fund to provide more structure to their giving. [A donor-advised fund is a charitable-giving vehicle administered by a third party to manage charitable donations on behalf of a family.] Each of my kids, aged 19 and 21, worked with a donor advisor and also attended a seminar to help them identify their philanthropic leanings. My daughter used her

*portion to sponsor raincoats for schoolchildren
living in the rain-soaked mountains of Ecuador.
My son, who played saxophone for his school
band, supported a music program at a local school
for at-risk children."*

GRATITUDE

Helping others opens your children's eyes to the fact that
not everyone lives the same way they do and teaches
them to be compassionate. It can also help put things
into perspective if they're developing a sense of entitlement. Gratitude doesn't seem to come naturally because
our minds resist making downward comparisons (upward
comparisons, as discussed earlier regarding social media
and FOMO, happen more naturally). Being grateful
takes practice until it becomes a habit.

THINGS TO DO

- Encourage and model an attitude of gratitude. Ask your kids what they're grateful for
  today or this week.
- Suggest they keep a gratitude journal to jot
  down each day (or each week) three things
  that happened that they're grateful for.

Invest

LONG-TERM INVESTING: START EARLY AND INVEST REGULARLY

Some people at this age, whether they're in university or working full-time, have more money than they need to cover their ongoing current expenses. The temptation is to see any extra funds as spending money, but it's a good idea to earmark some of it for investment. Emerging adults have decades ahead of them to invest, which gives them a huge advantage — time! Encourage your kid to start early and invest regularly, even if the amounts are small.

Emma Taylor began saving $5 each week when she was fifteen. Assuming Emma earned a 5 percent compound annual return, at 65 she would have $57,152. If she waited ten years and didn't start until age 25, she would have $32,978.34 at age 65. And if she waited even longer, until she was 35, and saved for 30 years, she would have only $18,137.81.

You can also consult the Compound Interest Calculator at www.getsmarteraboutmoney.ca/calculators/compound-interest-calculator.

When investing for a long-term goal, a much longer time horizon means you can choose investments with growth potential. Take advantage of time and let compounding work for you, as we saw in Chapter 4. Depending on your tolerance for risk, you may have many different investment options.

FAMILY DISCUSSION

Investments

Bonds:

- Explain that bonds are simply IOUs — they're debts issued by companies or governments.
- They usually pay a fixed or floating rate of interest to the investor for a specific period of time, called the "term."
- The interest rate is expressed as a percentage of the investment.
- Bonds issued by governments in the developed world are generally thought to be safe investments, and, if the government has a good track record, the interest rate you earn will be relatively low compared to bonds issued by entities that are considered riskier.
- Remember: low risk = low reward.

Stocks:

- Explain that stocks represent an ownership stake in a company.
- The owners of a company's stock are called shareholders.
- Some stocks are traded on public stock exchanges, and their prices are determined by buyers and sellers.
- Stock prices can be quite unpredictable

in the short run: they can go up or down, and there are no guarantees regarding the safety of your investment or the return of your original capital. You could double your money, lose your entire investment, or come out anywhere in between. For this reason, stocks are said to be risky.

- You wouldn't buy stocks if you were investing for a short-term goal: you won't have enough time to recover if the stock price falls drastically right before you need the money. The stock market meltdowns caused by the global financial crisis of 2008 and the economic shut-down triggered by the COVID-19 pandemic in 2020 are two noteworthy examples.

STOCKS, BONDS, AND OTHER INVESTMENTS

There are three traditional categories or classes of investments: cash, bonds, and stocks. There are also other types of investments, such as real estate, precious metals like gold and silver, and investments in private businesses. But when teaching your young adult, focus on the three traditional ones — the others are generally for more sophisticated investors with substantial investable assets.

In investing, there is a direct relationship between risk

and return. Lower-risk investments, like cash or bonds, have lower returns. Higher-risk investments, like stocks, have the potential to earn higher returns. Your child may have learned some of these concepts in a high school business class, but it doesn't hurt to review the basics if she shows interest.

Everyone has to assess their own comfort with risk. Some investors are very comfortable owning a high-risk portfolio, while others are very uncomfortable with the gyrations of the market and the possibility of losing their principal. But if you are willing to take some risk by owning stocks, the potential returns are also higher than they are with less risky investments like GICs or bonds. Most publicly traded stocks are also very liquid, meaning you can sell them at the prevailing market price quite quickly and easily.

When you own stocks, you can earn investment income in two ways: dividends and capital gains (or losses). Dividends represent a proportionate share of the profits of a company and are paid by some companies to their shareholders; the decision about whether to pay a dividend on common shares (and how much to pay) is made by a company's board of directors. A capital gain is the difference between what you pay for an investment and what you sell it for, less any transaction costs. If the difference is positive, you have a gain; if it's negative, you have a capital loss.

THINGS TO DO

Investment plan

Before moving on to the next steps of asset allocation and security selection, ask your child to answer the following three questions. Writing the answers down will help them create an investment plan:

- What are your investment objectives?
- What is your time horizon?
- What is your risk tolerance?

ASSET ALLOCATION AND SECURITY SELECTION

Once your young adult knows what he wants to achieve and when, he can decide how to achieve it with the proper asset allocation and securities. Asset allocation is the process of determining how the money in your investment portfolio should be divided among the different categories of investments: stocks, bonds, cash, real estate, and others. Getting the asset allocation right for the investor's circumstances is crucial because, according to the oft-quoted Brinson, Hood, and Beebower study,[15] it accounts for over 90 percent of the variability of the returns on a typical investor's portfolio. Contrary to popular belief, it's a much more

---

15. blogs.cfainstitute.org/investor/2012/02/16/setting-the-record-straight-on-asset-allocation/

important step than security selection. Security selection accounts for only 4.6 percent of the variability. But people tend to focus on picking stocks and other securities because it's "sexier" and may give them something to brag about!

FINTECH AND ROBO-ADVISORS

Innovation in financial services has led to the creation of "robo-advisors" (sometimes called digital portfolio managers), which are essentially software-driven investment management solutions that use technology to simplify every part of the investment process, including opening your account (onboarding), making regular contributions, portfolio construction, rebalancing, tax-loss harvesting and reporting. The use of technology (and the absence of traditional brick and mortar offices and branches) brings down the cost compared to traditional alternatives like full-service brokers.

Fintech has also made it possible to set up "money rules" to move, manage and save money automatically. For example, when your account balance rises above a chosen threshold, say $1,000, you can automatically move the surplus to a savings account. Or you can turn spending into saving or investing, by rounding up purchases made on your credit or debit card to the nearest dollar (or five dollars) and moving that difference to a savings or investment account.

RESPONSIBLE INVESTMENT

Young people today are environmentally and socially minded, and they want their investments to not only make money but to also make a positive impact on society. Responsible investment is an umbrella term for a broad range of approaches that can be used to incorporate environmental, social, and governance (ESG) considerations into the investment process. (It's sometimes also called sustainable investment.)

ESG integration refers to the environmental (e.g., pollution, clean water, climate change), social (e.g., human rights, gender equity, racial injustice, impact on community), and governance (e.g., board independence, conflicts of interest, ethical governing principles) factors of an investment that may have a material impact on its performance. Investments can be evaluated on ESG factors, along with more traditional financial measures.

Socially responsible investing (SRI) goes a step further, using ESG factors as either a negative or positive screen, actively eliminating or selecting investments according to specific ethical guidelines. Examples include avoiding investments in companies that harm the environment, make people sick, or violate human rights. It can also mean choosing companies that strive for gender equity or racial diversity. SRI lets young adults put their money where their values are and generate investment returns without violating their social conscience.

Finally, impact investing refers to investments made with the primary intention of generating a measurable, beneficial social or environmental impact. Making a positive financial return is a secondary concern.

A TALE OF THREE INVESTORS

The Taylors are moderate investors who are most comfortable with a balanced portfolio: 50 percent stocks, 40 percent bonds, and 10 percent cash.

Their friends the Bennetts have a greater appetite for risk and prefer to hold a more aggressive portfolio: 70 percent stocks, 20 percent bonds, and 10 percent cash.

Their friend Carol is widowed and is ultra-conservative. She's very risk averse, and although she will have a small pension, she's comfortable owning only GICs.

Let's assume that they each invest $100,000 and plan to reinvest any investment income they earn. How can we expect their portfolios to perform after 5 years, 10 years, and 20 years?

Generally, ultra-conservative portfolios will grow very slowly, and although there is no risk that you will lose your principal, there is a risk that the returns will not outpace inflation and that therefore you may outlive your money. This is in fact what happened to Carol. Although she was outperforming the other two portfolios after 5 years and staying even after 10, she fell far behind after 20 years. As the Taylors and the Bennetts experienced, a more aggressive asset mix means more growth potential but also more likelihood of experiencing losses. In this example, the stock market was volatile in the first ten years, and the more aggressive portfolios didn't really start to perform well until the second decade.

Investor	Portfolio	Initial Investment	After 5 years	After 10 years	After 20 years	Average Annual Return
Carol	Ultra-conservative	$100,000	$161,049	$236,206	$356,484	6.7%
Taylors	Balanced	$100,000	$154,330	$236,103	$424,785	7.5%
Bennetts	Aggressive	$100,000	$129,503	$236,736	$560,441	9.0%

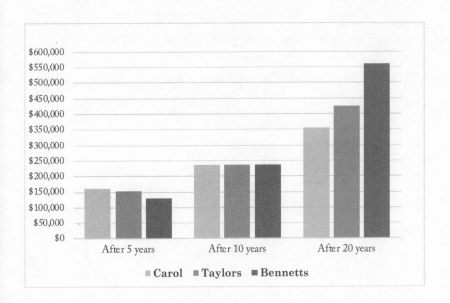

KEY POINTS

- Young adults become increasingly independent from you, but you can still have a lot of influence on them — they're often more willing to discuss important matters with you than they were just a few years earlier.
- Help them see that their newfound independence involves both privileges and responsibilities, i.e., they can work at more interesting jobs that pay them more, and as students they're entitled to certain tax breaks, but they have to file an income tax return to make sure they're taking full advantage of everything they're entitled to.
- Volunteering is a great way for young people to put their values into action, and it pays dividends in terms of real-world experience and personal satisfaction.
- It's a good idea to make sure they have basic investment knowledge. Some may already be in a position to start a portfolio; others will benefit from knowing what their options are when they do start to invest.
- Finally, the payoff from investing in your kids' financial education doesn't end when they become young adults. It continues, as you find yourself learning from them!

RESOURCES

Post-Secondary Student Budget

BUDGET CALCULATOR

This form will take about five minutes to complete. Please fill in as many of the fields below as possible with after-tax amounts to ensure an accurate estimate of the total budget you'll need.

INCOME Record or estimate your annual after-tax income from the following sources.		
Income	**Monthly**	**Annually**
Salary / Wages	$	$
Self-employment / Business income	$	$
Scholarships / Bursaries	$	$
Parental contributions	$	$
Other	$	$
Total Income	**$**	**$**

EXPENSES

Estimate your expenses for the items listed, either as monthly or yearly values. If you are not sure how much to allocate for a given item, it may be helpful to record all your expenses for an entire month before returning to complete this form.

Food / Housing	Monthly	Annually
Food	$	$
Mortgage / rent	$	$
Other housing costs	$	$
Utilities	$	$
Moving costs	$	$
Other	$	$
Total Food and Housing	**$**	**$**
Transportation	**Monthly**	**Annually**
Car payments	$	$
Insurance / license / registration	$	$
Service / repairs / gasoline	$	$
Public transportation / parking	$	$
Other, e.g. car share or ride share	$	$
Total Transportation	**$**	**$**
Education	**Monthly**	**Annually**
Tuition	$	$
Books / subscriptions	$	$
Exam fees	$	$
Professional fees	$	$
Other	$	$
Total Education	**$**	**$**
Investments and Savings	**Monthly**	**Annually**
RRSP contributions	$	$
Other	$	$
Total Investments and Savings	**$**	**$**

Lifestyle / Loans	Monthly	Annually
Loan payments	$	$
Government student loan payments	$	$
Insurance	$	$
Uninsured health services	$	$
Clothing / dry cleaning / grooming	$	$
Leisure activities	$	$
Child care	$	$
Travel	$	$
Other	$	$
Total Lifestyle / Loans	**$**	**$**
Total Expenses	**$**	**$**

Connect with Me

The Wisest Investment: Teaching Your Kids to Be Responsible, Independent and Money-Smart for Life is available in hard copy, as an ebook and as an audio book. It makes the perfect gift for parents (and grandparents). It can also be used by companies and organizations in programs for their customers, clients and employees. Please contact us for more information on bulk sales, including discounts available, at **books@robintaub.com**.

We would love to hear from you! For feedback and to enquire about speaking engagements such as webinars, keynotes, breakout sessions and workshops, please contact us at:

EMAIL:

speaking@robintaub.com

WEBSITES:

robintaub.com

thewisestinvestment.com

SOCIAL MEDIA:

Robin Taub

List of Resources

Further Resources

Throughout the book, I have referred to some resources that will help you learn more about the different topics covered. However, because I'm constantly finding fantastic new ones, it made sense to move this list online, where I can update it regularly. Visit any time at **robintaub.com**. There's no registration or password needed. Other readers stop by often and have frequently made excellent suggestions for me to check out and add.

About
the Author

Robin Taub is definitely not your typical accountant! After beginning her career as an auditor at KPMG, and then a tax specialist at Ernst & Young, Robin left the traditional world of accounting behind. Seeking new challenges, she spent five years in the complex world of derivatives marketing at Citibank Canada. Today, Robin is a financial writer, speaker, consultant and bestselling author.

Robin graduated with a Bachelor of Commerce degree, with high distinction, from the Rotman School of Management at the University of Toronto and earned her Chartered Professional Accountant designation (CPA, CA) in 1989.

Robin puts her money where her mouth is. She has two children, a son and a daughter, who have provided a lot of the material and inspiration for her work.

For fun, she loves to snowboard, cycle and go to concerts. She even got backstage once and met Bruce Springsteen — and has been dining out on it ever since!

You can learn more about Robin by visiting **robintaub.com**.

Acknowledgments

I would like to thank the following people, who have helped me to make this book a reality:

- David Chilton, for creating The Chilton Method, a powerful approach to non-fiction book creation and marketing. The information David shared in this online course helped me create a book that was not just good, but great (if I do say so myself!)
- Erik Leijon, my editor, for his many insights and suggestions to make the book both timely and evergreen.
- My husband, Jonathan, for being my sounding board and encouraging me every step of the way.

But most of all, I want to thank my two children, Justin and Natalie, for providing the inspiration and material for this book!

— Robin Taub